JOURNEY TO THE ROCK: THE CLIMB

DEVOTIONAL

JOURNEY TO THE ROCK
BOOK 2

© 2024 All Nations International AZ

Authors and illustrators maintain ownership rights. Used by permission

Print ISBN: 978-1-955759-39-7

eBook ISBN: 978-1-955759-40-3

Authors: Rev. Agnes I Numer, Revs. Gordon & Teresa Skinner

Special contributions: A. Flores, F. Metchie, S. Alanwoko

Illustrated by: Rebecca Brogan, Larry Cole, David Chika Onoh, Jackson Muthoni, Teresa Skinner, George Thomas

For more information: is58mti@gmail.com

www.all-nations.org

Seldom Seen Press

"If you don't plant something, you want on your Farmland something you don't want will grow on it.

And again, even if you plant something you want and you don't carefully tend to it, something you don't want will still grow and suffocate the things you planted.

Look for the arrow for quizzes, puzzles and devotional entries.

🔐 *Answers are in the back of the book.*

CONTENTS

Introduction   vi
How do we demonstrate the Love of God?   vii

THE BEATITUDES

They have to like me — Just the way I am   3
Why do we have the Beatitudes?   4
The Beatitudes   6
Blessed are those who mourn   10
A Short Story   14
Devo Day 1   15

LORD, YOU HAVE ORDAINED PEACE FOR US

Lord, You Have Ordained Peace for Us   19
Review: Lord, You Have Ordained Peace   24
Devo Day 2:   28

CONFLICT REVOLUTION

Conflict Revolution   33
Review: Conflict Revolution   43
Devo Day 3:   48

PRAISE AND WORSHIP

Praise and Worship   55
Which Realm?   59
Realms of Worship   63
Praise and Worship - Part 2   65
Praise in Spiritual Warfare   70
Review: Praise and Worship   71
Devo Day 4:   74

SPIRITUAL WARFARE

Spiritual Warfare   83
The Warrior   97
The Captive   103
Review: Spiritual Warfare   113
Review: Spiritual Warfare - Part 2   115
Quiz: Spiritual Warfare   118
Devo Day 5:   122

IMPACT OF ISAIAH 58

Isaiah 58   129
Isaiah 58 - the Vision   133
The Impact of Isaiah 58   138
Review: Impact of Isaiah 58   155
Devo Day 6   159
Prophecy #1   162
Prophecy #2   164

Answer Key   166
Notes   172
Acknowledgements   177

Introduction

Why is this called **"the Climb?"**

When we have asked Jesus into our hearts and begin our relationship with Jesus, it is sweet. We call and He answers. But, we can't remain there. We must press into all that Jesus has for us. We must represent and demonstrate His love to others.

This is a process and takes steps, much like a mountain goat climbing up a mountain. As we mature, we will learn to have sure footing. We learn from our mistakes and we will learn compassion for others.

We have included six basic principles to help you on your **Journey to the Rock**. Who is "the Rock?" — Jesus is...

HOW DO WE DEMONSTRATE THE LOVE OF GOD?

How do we hear God's voice to know the needs of others? Inside we do not "feel" the Love of God. We have never experienced God's love for others.

How do we allow the Love of God to grow in our hearts?

Jesus said,

> *"By this shall all men know that ye are my disciples, if ye have love one to another."*
>
> JOHN 13:35

- Become aware of His Love and care for us.

- Experience His creative miracles for us.

- Become like Jesus, ask Him to have His heart of Love replace our heart of stone.

Let's study "the Climb" together.

THE BEATITUDES

THEY HAVE TO LIKE ME — JUST THE WAY I AM

Sometimes we say "They have to like me. That's the way I am. If they don't like the way I am, that's too bad." We need to realize it is Jesus who changes our lives. We try but we can't do it. We think we're changing our lives, but it shows up in our daily our attitudes. **The way we speak to one another and the way we treat one another.**

Let me introduce you to the real Jesus.

The Jesus Christ that God sent into the world because He so loved the world that He created – He wanted everyone in the world to know His son, Jesus. Today, this still is the heart of the Father. We look at this world and it is all chaos. When God brings His judgment – it's worse than chaos. What are we going to do?

One thing God requires of us – that we **be** like Jesus."

The Beatitudes show us where to begin.

WHY DO WE HAVE THE BEATITUDES?

We have the Beatitudes because God is teaching us to have the right attitude. **An attitude that reflects His love and nature...** not our love and nature.

It is difficult for human beings to have the right attitude. The only sure way that we could have the right attitudes is to have Jesus in us.

**It's not just Jesus in us, but it's His love...
that He must place in us.**

We can see what we call human love imperfect human love – the Bible calls it fleshly or carnal* love. But human love isn't sufficient to change our attitude. It takes God to change our attitudes. You might say, "You don't live around the

---

* Something related to the body or the flesh

people I live around. You don't know the people I know."
There's one cure, that's Jesus.

Not a half-way Jesus, but Jesus all the way.

That we might love with His love in everything!

The Beatitudes are for us to live by. They are not just scriptures for us to get to heaven. They are for us to live by.

Let's stop for a moment and consider our attitudes:

Do we represent Jesus, or do we represent our flesh?

_____

_____

_____

_____

_____

_____

_____

_____

_____

_____

_____

_____

_____

_____

THE BEATITUDES

And seeing the multitudes, He went up on a mountain, and when He was seated His disciples came to Him. 2 Then He opened His mouth and taught them, saying:

3 "Blessed are the poor in spirit,

For theirs is the kingdom of heaven.

4 Blessed are those who mourn,

For they shall be comforted.

5 Blessed are the meek,

For they shall inherit the earth.

6 Blessed are those who hunger and thirst for righteousness,

For they shall be filled.

7 Blessed are the merciful,

For they shall obtain mercy.

8 Blessed are the pure in heart,

For they shall see God.

9 Blessed are the peacemakers,

For they shall be called sons of God.

10 Blessed are those who are persecuted for righteousness' sake,

For theirs is the kingdom of heaven.

11 Blessed are you when they revile and persecute you, and say all kinds of evil against you falsely for My sake.

12 Rejoice and be exceedingly glad, for great is your reward in heaven, for so they persecuted the prophets who were before you.

This scripture matches the picture story. Share the story in your own words.

Which Beatitude is missing?

2.

3.

?

7.

JESUS

BLESSED ARE THOSE WHO MOURN

Blessed are those who mourn, for they shall be comforted.

Many times we face difficult circumstances.

Maybe it is the loss of a loved one, the loss of a job, a home. Things that we feel identify our worth, our identity, our love and respect for ourselves.

Jesus cares about those circumstances and how they affect our lives. He loves us and cares deeply for us. He created us and cherishes who He has created us to be.

When we grieve over our losses, we may feel angry or we may feel sad, or depressed. By realizing Jesus cares and already has a plan for the next step, give your heart and emotions to Him and let Him guide you through this valley, this sadness, this loss.

One time a friend and mentor very close to me died. I was so sad and felt I really missed her. It was as if I heard these words, "Yes, I have also missed her all these years." I realized that Jesus loved my friend more than I ever could. And that He missed her while she was on this earth, and now she would be with him. I would someday go to be with them and we would be together forever. Never would we separate again.

Will you spend eternity with Jesus? He wants you to. He loves you more than you know.

Would you allow Jesus to comfort you now?

A SHORT STORY

Blessed are those who hunger and thirst for righteousness, For they shall be filled.

When I first met the Lord I knew that I had a problem. I knew I was not a Faithful person and wondered if I could be faithful to Jesus.

I asked my pastor "How can I learn to be obedient to the Lord?" She said, "By obeying." That was not the answer I was looking for. I actually did not understand it.

But as I matured in the Lord I realized that He would be Faithful through us, and as we obeyed each little request from Him. As we saw others needs and allowed Him to meet those needs through us.

We would learn faithfulness. Is there an area in your life where God has asked you to do something? How will you obey Him?

DEVO DAY 1

CONSIDER OUR ATTITUDES

Define these words from Matthew 5

Poor in spirit
mourn
meek
righteousness
merciful
peacemakers
persecuted
pure in heart

Study and write the Greek meaning for these words

kingdom[1] of heaven[2]
comforted[3]
inherit the earth[4]
filled[5]
obtain mercy [6]

pure[7] in heart[8]
shall see[9] God[10]
children[11] of God
righteousness' sake[12]

Greek meanings are in the back of the book.

Afterthought: Let's STOP and consider our attitudes: Do we represent Jesus, or have we been representing ourselves and our fleshly attitudes?

Journal entry:

Which of these "beatitudes" are in your life right now? How can we integrate the Beatitudes into our daily lives?

_____

_____

_____

_____

_____

_____

_____

_____

_____

_____

_____

_____

_____

_____

LORD, YOU HAVE ORDAINED PEACE FOR US

LORD, YOU HAVE ORDAINED PEACE FOR US

"Lord, thou wilt ordain peace for us: for thou also hast wrought all our works in us. O Lord our God, other lords beside thee have had dominion over us: but by thee only will we make mention of thy name. They are dead, they shall not live; they are deceased, they shall not rise: therefore hast thou visited and destroyed them, and made all their memory to perish."

ISAIAH 26:12 KJV

Lord, You will **ordain peace** for us...

Why did he say it that way? He said it because He willed it, He desires it for us – but it is up to us to receive it. He said, "I will that you have peace." If He has ordained peace for us, then we have to receive that peace. He has also **wrought** – which is to beat out or shape all of our works in us... everything that we are He will make us. If we let Him.

It is not our will that gives us power to have peace - we can only have it if we can accept it. If we worry instead of accepting His peace then we will not have peace. Other lords rob us of that peace. Jesus said, "I give my peace to you" but if we do not receive it – how can we have it. If you have other lords in your life you will not have peace in your life.

Before we can have God's peace we have to clean house by acknowledging the other lords and then by renouncing them. "O Lord our God, other lords beside thee have had dominion over us: but by thee only will we make mention of thy name." We are not going to make mention of those other lords any more, we are going to renounce them we will formally declare that we have abandoned them. And then... we don't mention them anymore.

God said, "They are dead, they shall not live; they are deceased, they shall not rise: therefore hast thou visited and destroyed them, and made all their memory to perish." God took those former lords and destroyed them! If we will just allow Jesus to take those lords and destroy them God will cause their memory to perish – we will not remember the horrible things anymore. We will have His peace. He will change our life and gives us His peace. Jesus said to the storm "Peace be still." The Holy Spirit gave His Peace through the disciples when they ministered to the people. If the people received their word then peace remained. If the people rejected their word, then Jesus said,

"You shake the dust off of your feet." (Matthew 10:13.14)

Jesus gives us this peace today. People must receive truth in order for their lives to change, if they reject the truth, they will not have peace anymore. If you lose your peace, ask yourself where you were when you lost it? What were you doing? What was God telling you to do? Go back to that place and find your peace again. God says, I give you my peace, not as the world gives. Let not your heart be troubled, put your trust in me, for I am the light of the world.

If you are out somewhere and you do not feel God's peace – stop and ask God what happened? Obey God, you do not want to be where God is not. We have to have perfect peace to move forward and do what God wants us to do. If we have both truth and deception – we have confusion. How are we going to know what we are supposed to do? How will we lead others?

Does the church realize we can be filled with His perfect peace? The world wants their way, but Jesus wants us to come to the light. If others reject the truth they will be deceived, but we will stand with boldness and we will have His perfect peace.

SOMETIMES WHEN THE DEVIL SPEAKS TO US HE TRIES TO MAKE US DOUBT; DO NOT LISTEN TO HIM!

Sometimes when the devil speaks to us he tries to make us doubt; do not listen to him! Tell him, "You do not live in me anymore!" **You do not need to argue with the devil,** you do not need to be afraid. God's word is in us and He is the one that keeps us from fear. There is no law against truth, love and peace: no one and no law can take it from you. When we believe God's word then the devil cannot have any effect on us. Testing will come and that is when we must stand on God's word. He will use the testing to make us strong. When Jesus was tested He said, "It is written." He was victor over the enemy and so are we because we believe in His truth.

God ordained peace for us, He has taken us through, we have stood in the truth, and now God can use us to help someone else.

Oh Lord our God, only by thee will we make mention of thy name – the former lords are dead – if they are deceased, they are dead. If we try to dig up the past, we are digging up dead bodies. They are gone. As we allow God to take His perfect peace in us, **the former lords no longer live.** He ordained it, He desires it and He willed it for us. Whatever is in His will is yours – what are you going to do with it?

Where do we get the truth? From His word. How do you know you have the truth? Jesus said, "I am the way the truth and light." He is the Way back the Father. There is no other way. In the new birth **the Prince of Peace comes to live inside of us.** If we confess our sin He will forgive us and give us His peace, His life, His love and fill us with His light. Then we realize our sins are gone and perfect peace is there. His written word must be strong in us! Jesus is the Living Word in us.

God wants to use you to help others. After He has brought this peace in your life. He wants to use you as a light in this world for others.

Discern the need that they have, the area of their life that does not have peace. Let them read Isaiah 26 and know that this is god's will for them. That Jesus died and rose again, that they may have peace and eternal life. Pray with them believing for this creative miracle in their mind, their emotions and their spirit. God will heal their brokenness, and He will visit those areas of torment and bring peace. He will show them how to allow Him to make them into a man or woman of God. Show them to read His word and get to know him.

Encourage them to stay away and not go places or do things where those former lords had control.

This is something God does, **only God can bring this kind of peace,** peace that passes understanding. We cannot deliver someone from torment only He can. And when He does oh the glory! Oh, the joy! We are set free.

God wills peace for you, He desires it for you... are you ready to receive His peace now?

REVIEW: LORD, YOU HAVE ORDAINED PEACE

1. We have the power to have peace by ourselves
a. True
b. False

2. God has made a way for us to have peace by:
a. Worrying about it
b. Trying harder to have it
c. Accepting the peace He offers us

3. To have peace we must get rid of other lords by:
a. Renouncing them
b. Continually talking to them
c. Wrestling with them until morning

4. In order for our life to change we must:
a. Read more 'how to' books
b. Often be defeated
c. Receive the truth

5. We do not need to be afraid of the devil because
a. We don't know his future judgement
b. God's word is in us and He is the one that keeps us from fear
c. We have a cross around our neck

6. Once God has taken us through, and we have the victory we can help someone else
a. True
b. False

7. Testing will come and make us weaker
a. True
b. False

8. The former Lords are dead, they are deceased and can no longer affect us unless:
a. We fellowship with godly friends
b. We worship too long at one time
c. We dig up the past or we live in sin

9. We can help other people by letting them know God wants them to have peace
a. True
b. False

10. We can deliver someone else from torment, and we can give them this peace
a. True
b. False

The LORD
is close to the brokenhearted
and saves those who are crushed in spirit.
— Psalm 34:18

Come to me, all you who are weary and burdened,
and I will give you rest. Take my yoke upon you and
for I am gentle and humble in heart, and you will fir
For my yoke is easy and my burden is light. — Ma   instead
                                                                              of praise
       Cast all your anxiety on him   I have loved you
because he cares for you.   with an everlasting lov
                              I have drawn you with i.
       — 1 Peter 5:7   I will build you up again a

                                                              — Jer
Never will I leave you;
Never will I forsake you.

   — Hebrews 13:5

om me,
r your souls.
28-30

...whoever comes to me
I will never drive away.
— John 6:37

The Spirit of the Sovereign LORD is on me...
He has sent me to bind up the brokenhearted,
proclaim freedom for the captives and release from darkness
e prisoners... to comfort all who mourn, and provide
ho grieve in Zion — to bestow on them a crown of beauty
the oil of gladness instead of mourning, and a garment
f a spirit of despair. — Isaiah 61:1-3
indness.

will be rebuilt.
1:3-4

For I am convinced
that neither death nor life,
neither angels nor demons,
neither the present nor the future,
nor any powers, neither
height nor depth, nor
anything else in all
creation will be able
to separate us from
the love of God
that is in
Christ Jesus
our Lord.
— Romans
8:38-39

DEVO DAY 2:

LORD, YOU HAVE ORDAINED PEACE FOR US

God has an incredible way of delivering us from our past. Our minds are like a recorder. But when God visits those areas in our minds and brings deliverance, only He can erase that recording of the event that happened to us.

I have found that the only reason it comes back to my mind is to share with others how God delivered me.

Forgiveness is critical to be free from tormenting thoughts.

Has someone harmed you? Do you feel bitterness inside because of what they have done, or what they should have done?

One time when I in India, my mind was continually tormented by the memory of a person who had done something very wrong to me.

I could not forget the person and I was always thinking of them and what they had done.

On this trip, where I was in India, they had a lot of mosquitos. Those mosquitos would always find me and bite me. Even when I had made sure I cleared every mosquito from my mosquito net that covered my bed, as soon as I would try to sleep, I would hear the buzzing of the mosquito — so loudly, right in my ear.

I had allowed myself to become so bitter. Very frustrated one day, I cried out to the Lord and said, **"Why does this person bother my mind so much? They are like a mosquito!"**

I heard God clearly say, "Well, what do you do with mosquitos?"

In my bitterness I replied, "What do you mean? What do I do with mosquitos?" God did not answer me... He was quiet.

Exasperated I replied, "I spray them with '6/12', that what I do with mosquitos." He did not answer me... He was quiet.

It is so dangerous to allow ourselves to become bitter. This is why God says to not allow the sun to go down on our anger. When we allow it to fester in our hearts and minds, we become bitter and insensitive to God and His desire for our lives.

Again, exasperated I cried out to God, "Ok, what do you want me to do with '6/12'? Ok, I will look it up in the Bible. Where do I look?" I was so wrong; my attitude was so wrong... I was so blessed that we serve a forgiving God. Still, He would not answer. **The quietness was so loud.**

I took my Bible, "Ok," I said to God. I was still exasperated. "Which chapter do I look in? Ok, I will just choose one. I will look in Matthew, Matthew 6:12."

Angrily, I grabbed my Bible, opened it and read:

And forgive us our debts, as we forgive our debtors.

Matthew 6:12

I was shocked. It shocked me so much that all anger left me. I realized how much God had forgiven me and I must forgive this person. I realized if I could not forgive this person, God could not forgive me.

That day God gave me the strength to do something I could not do on my own. I bowed myself before God and said, "God I cannot forgive this person, but because you are asking me to do this, with my will, I forgive them." Immediately I felt peace and felt like myself again. The stink of that person's memory left me.

I only remember this story when I am to share it with others.

I have peace.

God will truly:

"Visit them and make their memory to perish."

If we let Him.

If we yield to Him.

CONFLICT REVOLUTION

CONFLICT REVOLUTION

Our goals can be more than winning an argument or finding out who is right and who is wrong. Our greatest goal is to believe God that through the conflict there can be a "Revolution"

Revolution definition:

A radical and pervasive change in society and the social structure, especially one made suddenly and often accompanied by violence.

A sudden, extreme, or complete change in the way people live, work, think, etc.

Conflicts are typically not much fun. They can threaten to bring a negative change. They can come up suddenly and unexpectedly. They can lead to breakup of a relationship **OR** they can lead to a radical and powerful change toward deeper relationship; more respect, trust and understanding. **Conflict can be the quickest way to positive changes.** Do not be afraid of conflict. Learn that it is **how we act and respond** which can cause conflicts to bring a much needed "Revolution."

Look at every conflict as an **opportunity:**

- To deepen the relationship.
- To understand one another better, be closer and more open.
- To earn mutual respect.

GUIDE TO POSITIVE REVOLUTION DURING A CONFLICT

We are on the same side.

Take the attitude that **this problem is not going to divide us.**

Physically position yourselves so you are both together, facing the problem.

Being seated is a non-threatening position.

Have an attitude of Humility

How have **I** contributed to the problem? **Humility can admit** that I am part of the problem.

Humility can say, **"I'm sorry, forgive me."**

PICK THE TIME AND PLACE TO TALK.

It is not a good time to solve issues when you are too angry. Take time to cool down.

Pick a good place. Not in front of children or other people who do not need to be involved.

- **I value our Relationship.**

Take the time to express your value for the relationship and that you hope to find a solution to the problem at hand.

What is the problem we are trying to solve?

If you can both agree to define the problem you have a chance to solve it.

- **Express your true feelings and listen for what they are really feeling.**

Reflect what they have said by saying, "Let me see if I understand, are you saying that..... or, are you feeling....."

Seek to truly understand.

Not listening just to their words but to their heart.

Listen Well.

Often if you listen well you will get an opportunity to speak and be heard.

Let them know you are listening by your body language and your responses.

Use active listening. "I hear you, I think I understand what you are saying," etc.

Seek Solutions together.

Can we look to God's Word together for an answer? If His word is respected, He has an answer.

HERE ARE 10 PRINCIPLES TO HELP US DEVELOP DEEPER RELATIONSHIPS:

1. HEALING OF THE PAST.

a. When we have been hurt by something in our past which has not yet been healed and someone does something which "feels" similar we can get a flashback of emotions and memories which can cause us to overreact. Our memories can strongly affect our present relationships if we do not forgive and allow God to heal us by His Spirit. God can use current situations to "stir up" old hurts. If we are alert this is a good time to face the past hurts and let Him heal us.

2. GOD'S LOVE, NOT MAN'S LOVE.

a. Our human love can only go so far. God's love never ends and never gives up. People really need God's love and not our sympathy. We can often be too hard when people need a firm answer and too hard when they really need love and encouragement. Let God love through you. This begins by allowing God's love to penetrate our own hearts. We need a revelation of how much he loves us. Feelings of rejection and abandonment which we have will often be projected onto others when it's not even true.

3. VOWS ARE FOREVER. THEY ARE A PROMISE AND A COMMITMENT.

a. Go ahead, **pull out your old wedding vows.** Read them over carefully. Let yourself realize that vow is really a commitment... "'till death do us part". There is such a comfort in knowing that we are going to work together to make this work.

b. **Divorce is not an option. Never even bring up that word.** Don't let it be in your vocabulary or in your mind. Never use it as a threat. Especially when you believe that God joined you together you will not let anyone or anything tear you asunder.

4. TEMPTATIONS ARE PARASITES.

a. There are vices and habits and addictions which are as destructive as termites and parasites.

i. When the human body is ravaged by parasites nothing will work right. There is a lot of pain, and the body is sick. It is the same in a marriage.

ii. **Parasites kill.** What begins small can grow and take over the whole relationship and bring its destruction if not treated correctly.

iii. We must get rid of habits and addictions which threaten to destroy:

1. Confess your fault to God.

2. **Seek an accountability partner.**

3. Cry out to God for his power to help you overcome.

4. Do not give up on your first try to overcome. Get up and keep pressing in.

5. WALKING IN FORGIVENESS.

a. With God we know that **He is Forgiving.** We can be sure that when we come to Him humbly confessing our sin that He will accept us, He will forgive us and love us.

b. When we walk in love, we walk in forgiveness. We do not decide each time... "will I forgive this time?" Jesus said seventy times seven. When we hold on to things and count how many times... then we are not walking in forgiveness.

c. Revenge must be left to God. When we are angry, we are tempted to hurt others with our words and actions. Leave the revenge to God. Do not take it into your own hands.

6. HONOR, RESPECT, LOVE CHERISH.

a. Define these words - Honor, Respect, Love Cherish

b. Men need to be **Respected and Honored.**

i. Learn how to demonstrate respect.

ii. A woman causes all her children to respect or disrespect her man.

iii. What is important is how you say something more than what you say.

iv. Choose to never speak badly about your mate in public or to your friends. Build them up, honor them and make them special.

a. **Women need to be loved**, cherished and nourished. Look at it like a garden that needs to be watered and tended to bring forth fruit.

i. Each woman hears, "I love you" in a different way.

ii. Learn the best ways to say, "I love you" to her.

iii. Make her feel special.

iv. **Speak well of her in private and in public.**

v. Be creative. The fact that you took the time to notice, the trouble to do something, and the care to make it special mean so much.

7. WALK IN HUMILITY WITH EACH OTHER.

a. Men, learn to say, "I am sorry, I was wrong"

b. Women learn to say, "I forgive you" and accept the apology. Let it go. **Do not bring it up again next argument.**

8. Treat others like they are going to be... Not the way they may be today.

a. See others the way that God sees them. **This takes faith...** see the potential He sees.

b. Don't constantly nag, let God control others and not you.

c. Be patient while He is working. God's not finished with them yet.

9. RESPOND BY THE SPIRIT OF THE LORD NOT REACT BY THE FLESH.

a. As we learn to walk in the Spirit, **we will not fulfill the desires of our flesh.** There are times we would just love to just react and "let them have it" or "blow off steam" and "give them what they deserve". All of these things would be giving into our flesh instead of giving His Spirit the right to control our tongue and our emotions.

b. When we respond by His Spirit then He will deal with them Himself.

c. A soft answer turns away wrath; but grievous answer stirs up wrath.

10. UNCONDITIONAL LOVE.

Unconditional synonyms: wholehearted, unqualified, unreserved, unlimited, unrestricted, unmitigated, unquestioning, total, entire, full, absolute, out-and-out, unequivocal.

Unconditional love is what God demonstrates to us. Even while we were still sinners Christ died for us. **The worthy died for the unworthy.** He did not look at our condition as impossible. He reached out in hope that He could touch and change our lives.

a. When we love someone with unconditional love we will find that we cannot do it in our own strength. The ability to love unconditionally only comes from realizing that we have needed unconditional love ourselves. When we realize how much He loves us we can begin to love like He has loved us.

b. **Unconditional love is given freely,** without demanding anything in return. This goes against our fleshly nature.

c. The power of unconditional love is that it is given freely. It is a choice to love.

d. This kind of love is **life changing for both people** involved.

e. It takes faith to love unconditionally, and God will see and answer. **God will bring the changes needed.**

Relationships are so rewarding. People add joy and fulfillment to our lives. They can give us so much happiness and pain. Relationships are also hard work. It takes commitment and wisdom. God gives us the Holy Spirit to help us when we need more grace.

Have you ever wondered some time when you prayed for more patience and grace if He specially sent certain people into your life to develop those virtues you were praying for? We cannot love those people without His help. So, we must call out to Him. When He adds more patience then we can be more patient with everyone around us. Once He has given His gifts to us, they are ours. This is how we grow. From Grace to Grace.

2 Peter 1:5-7 And beside this, giving all diligence, add to your faith virtue; and to virtue knowledge; 6 And to knowledge temperance; and to temperance patience; and to patience

godliness; 7 And to godliness **brotherly kindness;** and to brotherly kindness, **charity.**

God develops His character in us as we meet people who challenge us. This is a progression from faith, to temperance, to brotherly kindness and finally on to charity... which is God's unconditional love through us. He says we must **give all diligence** to add His character to ourselves. Please accept the invitation to grow in His character and graces through conflict and difficult people.

Tips for Arguing Fairly

1. Make sure you have enough time to discuss your disagreement.
2. Don't react. Respond by the Spirit of the Lord.
3. Stay to the point. Listen Respectfully.
4. Don't attack the other person's character.
5. Don't bring up the past.
6. Don't argue with an angry person, let them cool down first.
7. Not in front of the children, congregation or others.
8. Always Honor.
9. Always make up later.
10. Choose your battles.
11. Don't go to bed angry.

If we allow Him, God will help us to turn every Conflict into a Revolution in our own life and in our relationships.

REVIEW: CONFLICT REVOLUTION

DISCUSSION QUESTIONS

Describe how God works through relationships to develop His character in us.

Define Conflict Revolution in your own words

Define these four words: Love, Cherish, Respect and Honor

Describe two ways you might show respect to a man that could be meaningful to him?

Describe two ways you might show love to a woman that could be most meaningful to her?

Explain how can hurts of the past affect today? Tell of one experience where this has happened to you.

1. Form 2 groups and practice together (or in pairs) saying, "I am sorry, I was wrong." In this group exercise we will have the men "practice" apologizing and the women will graciously accept that apology. This can be uncomfortable at first.

That is why practice is needed. If you are doing this alone, find someone during the day to apologize to. We all offend others so we should be able to find someone.

2. Whose responsibility is it to change other people we are close to?

3. What is our responsibility?

This would be a good time to repent for taking God's job

REVIEW

1. A sudden, extreme change in the way people live, work, think, etc. is called:
a. A conflict
b. A revolution
c. A deal breaker
d. An act of humility

2. An uncomfortable conflict can be the quickest way to positive changes
a. True
b. False

3. Conflicts can lead toward a deeper, more trusting relationship
a. True
b. False

4. A conflict can be an opportunity to:
a. Earn mutual respect

b. Pay the mortgage

c. Make the person pay what they owe you

d. All of the above

5. If you spent too much time listening you will never be able to get your point across

a. True

b. False

6. Select 3 principles that help develop deeper relationships

a. Allow deep sympathy for the person to invade your heart

b. Let God heal you from past issues which arise in present conflicts

c. Learn to love with God's love

d. Realize how habits and addictions are affecting your relationships

e. Nurture your feelings of rejection and abandonment

f. Feel sorry for yourself

7. At a wedding the most important thing is:

a. The wedding cake

b. The color of the dresses

c. The vows you make

d. The kind of pastor who officiates the wedding

8. When we walk in forgiveness, we have to decide each time whether to forgive or not.

a. True

b. False

9. Women will flourish fruitfully if you nourish them like a garden that needs to be watered and cared for
a. True
b. False

10. Keep bringing up the past until you have resolved it
a. True
b. False

11. Humility treats people the way they are today
a. True
b. False

12. Choose 4 words which define unconditional love
a. Wholehearted
b. Partiality
c. Unrestricted
d. Unlimited
e. Doubtful
f. Suspicious
g. Unreserved

13. It is never OK to disagree and argue
a. True
b. False

14. Choose 4 points to argue fairly
a. Ramble on and on
b. Listen respectfully
c. Stay to the point. Don't get sidetracked
d. Bring up the past
e. Attack the person

f. Respond, don't react

g. Don't argue when angry

h. Call them bad names

15. When we have said or done something hurtful what should we say?

a. The devil made me do it

b. It is partly your fault

c. I am sorry, I was wrong

d. None of the above

16. Whose responsibility is it to change the person we are close to?

a. His

b. Hers

c. Theirs

d. God's

DEVO DAY 3:
CAN WE TALK?

"I'm going to beat up my wife really bad; I need to teach her a lesson," fumed Michael.

"Hey, man, where did that come from?" Steven replied in shock.

"She hurt me, and this is not the first time; I've got to give her a piece of my mind," Michael retorted.

"Come on, man, let it go. That's not a legitimate fight for you. Leave it alone!" replied Steve.

When we study 1 Timothy 6:12, we discover that the "Fight of Faith" is the only legitimate fight for the Christian.

This is not a fight with people.

> *For we do not wrestle against flesh and blood, but*
> *against principalities, against powers, against*

the rulers of the darkness of this age, against
spiritual hosts of wickedness in the heavenly
places.

EPHESIANS 6:12 NIV

Fighting with people generally is wrong. Try to avoid arguing, striving and working against others. Sometimes, it might seem right just to 'fight' for something you perceive requires fighting. Maybe to protect your family, your country, your children. Seek the Lord's guidance first.

Remember as Christians, the Bible compelled us to live the higher life by resolving the disagreement and speaking kindly to each other.

Now therefore, it is already an utter failure for
you that you go to law against one another.
Why do you not rather accept wrong? Why
do you not rather let yourselves be cheated?

1 CORINTHIANS 6:7

In Ephesians Paul likens the relationship between husband and wife with the relationship between Christ and the Church. There are no irreconcilable differences. This relationship is sacrificial, and it is giving.

In relationships with others, consider Abraham, who when he had dispute with his nephew, Lot, resolved it without a squabble.

So Abram said to Lot, "Let's not have any
quarreling between you and me, or between
your herders and mine, for we are close
relatives.

GENESIS 13:8 NIV

Remember, our spouse or family members may also be Christians and share the same love from our heavenly Father. And if they are not, Jesus tells us to be light to them.

We shouldn't believe that being calm enough to settle conflicts without resorting to fighting or bitterness puts us at a disadvantage. We must choose to think love, think heavenly, and when we do, there is no need to fight for anything.

Jesus chose to resolve conflicts with His love.

After reading this, write in your journal what changes would you make in future disagreements?

Journal

Think outside the box

PRAISE AND WORSHIP

PRAISE AND WORSHIP

SINGING WITHOUT GOD'S ANOINTING – IS JUST SINGING.

"It is a fearful thing to produce 'Praise and Worship' music that leads into hunger for more music – worship must lead to a hunger for the depths of God and His word. As worship leaders we are taking the chance that the general public may or may not like the music that God prophesies through us...but it is more important to please God. We know the place that the enemy had was to bring praises before the throne. How careful we must be that we will not fall like he did and long for that praise for ourselves."

In the old testament the Holy of Holies was hidden by a veil. The only time anyone was allowed to enter was once a year on the Holy Day Yom Kippur. Only the High Priest entered and offered blood sacrifices and burned incense before the Mercy Seat.

. . .

Today, as Musicians we are also considered priests.

Why do we want to enter the Holy of Holies?

The office of the priest was a hereditary role. The priest spent his entire life serving God and offering sacrifices to ask forgiveness for God's people. Some priests were the most wicked men in the nation, instead of crying out against sin, they joined into sin. As musicians let us guard our hearts, that we may carry God's presence to His people that they may come into His presence for healing, restoration and the forgiveness of sin. Let us praise and worship with a pure heart without shame and without shaming God.

Before the priest went into the Holy of Holies, he sanctified himself. He set himself aside and asked God to cleanse him from his sin and remove anything that would offend God. Sanctification identifies us with God, who is separate from this world. The priest wore special garments with beautiful colors with gold, blue, purple and scarlet.

May we see the Worship Leader as a priest before God?

Who is the Worshiper?

The worshiper is not only those singing in front. The people we sing to will also worship God. We do not bring others into the presence of God. We worship God and as His

56

presence fills the room, people choose to enter or do not choose to enter in.

LEADING WORSHIP

As a worship leader we discern the Heart of our Father God and praise Him – as we worship God, God brings His people into His presence, and He compels our hearts into a deeper commitment.

As worship leaders our devotion to God and our love for God shows through our worship. We cannot pretend, our skill can hide how deep our relationship is with God. It is to that extent that we will express worship.

Why do we want to enter into God's intimate presence?

So that they will long to live there – forever, forsaking sin and all other gods. Desiring to be the bride of Christ, not just remaining a disciple. That their hearts may become open to receive the rest of the service, the word of God through the Pastor or the ministry that will be given after the song service.

As we chose to worship, God strengthens us to pass through everything.

Remember Paul singing in prison?

And when they had laid many stripes on them,

*they threw them into prison, commanding
the jailer to keep them securely. Having
received such a charge, he put them into the
inner prison and fastened their feet in the
stocks.*

ACTS 16:23-25

Man is made with a soul, a spirit and our body. Our soul
consists of our mind, will and emotions. Our spirit comes
from God and relates to God. Our body is where we live.
This helps us to understand how we worship.

WHICH REALM?

What realm do the music you play and the songs you sing take your listeners into?

WHICH REALM DOES THE MUSIC YOU PLAY AND THE SONGS THAT YOU SING LEAD THOSE LISTENING INTO?

A good guideline for praise and worship is to realize that we are only accompanying what God is doing.

We must realize that we are created to praise God.

We come before Him with a pure heart.

Come expecting God to move.

When God moves... flow with Him.

Our responsibility is to compliment God not to expect God to assist us.

We are priests before Him. Worship Him in spirit and in truth not bringing shame to Him but bringing His people before Him that He may remove their shame.

Anticipate that God will move among His people He inhabits the praises of His people and when God moves - we change.

Worship God in Spirit and in truth. Purify your heart before you start playing. Bring your praise as an offering before Him. If you have any sin, or anything against anyone take care of it before you worship. Ask for forgiveness clear the disagreement. That you may be a priest before Him.

Practice **before you play**. Practice your instrument, practice playing and singing as a group. Make sure that those engineering your team have all of the amplification equipment ready before you worship. Don't allow team members to practice during worship. We do not want to be a distraction - we want to worship God.

The focus is on God not on ourselves.

Praise ye the LORD. Praise God in his sanctuary: praise him in the firmament of his power.
Praise him for his mighty acts: praise him according to his excellent greatness.
Praise him with the sound of the trumpet: praise him with the psaltery and harp.
Praise him with the timbrel and dance: praise him with stringed instruments and organs.
Praise him upon the loud cymbals: praise him upon the high sounding cymbals.
Let every thing that hath breath praise the LORD. **Praise ye the LORD.**

PSALMS 150:1-6

THERE ARE DIFFERENT REALMS OF PRAISE AND WORSHIP.

THE SOULISH REALM

Music can move people. It moves people to dance, to sing, to "fall in love," to be depressed, to be happy.

Most music is performed in the soulish realm. Its purpose is to entertain. But does this music compel our hearts to enter into God's presence?

THE REALM OF PRAISE

Praise begins to minister to the Spirit man. This music begins to compel the heart to focus on God rather than self. The Spirit of God begins to move in the hearts of people, He may bring healing, deliverance and other gifts of the Spirit.

Sing to the Lord a new song,
And His praise in the assembly of saints.

Let Israel rejoice in their Maker;
Let the children of Zion be joyful in their King.
Let them praise His name with the dance;
Let them sing praises to Him with the timbrel
*   and harp.*
For the Lord takes pleasure in His people;
He will beautify the humble with salvation.
Let the saints be joyful in glory;
Let them sing aloud on their beds.

PSALMS 149:1-5

THE REALM OF WORSHIP

When the worship leader discerns the Heart of the God and worships Him, **God brings His people into His presence.**

When we enter into God's presence through worship our lives change. We enter into His presence abandoning our worries, concerns and appointments, our focus is on God alone. We realize God's greatness, His love and who He is. It is in this place that God speaks to our hearts giving us healing, direction and peace. It is in this realm that we become so aware of Him.

We cannot be afraid to enter into intimate worship of God in front of others. It is only by entering into this place of intimate worship that we can lead others to the freedom of expressing their love to their Heavenly Father.

Praise in Spiritual Warfare

When we look at King Jehoshaphat we see an incredible situation:

> *Now when they began to sing and to praise, the Lord set ambushes against the people of Ammon, Moab, and Mount Seir, who had come against Judah; and they were defeated.*

2 CHRONICLES 20:22

We see here that as God's people not just sang but praised Him, He destroyed the enemy. There are times that God uses our praise as Spiritual Warfare.

> *Let the high praises of God be in their mouth, And a two-edged sword in their hand, To execute vengeance on the nations, And punishments on the peoples; To bind their kings with chains, And their nobles with fetters of iron; To execute on them the written judgment— This honor have all His saints.*

PSALM 149:6-9 NKJV

WHEN WE SING THE ENEMY FLEES.

REVIEW: PRAISE AND WORSHIP

1. Singing without God's anointing – is just singing.
a. True
b. False

2. Musicians are not considered priests.
a. True
b. False

3. Lucifer used to bring praises before the throne.
a. True
b. False

4. As musicians let us _____ our hearts, that we may carry God's _____ to His people that they may receive _____, _____ and the forgiveness of sin.

5. Let us praise and worship with a _____ _____ without _____ and without shaming God.

6. Before the priest went into the Holy of Holies, he sanctified himself. Should we sanctify ourselves before worship?
a. Yes
b. No
c. Sometimes

7. Our love for God shows through our worship
a. True
b. False

8. We can pretend, our skill will hide how deep our relationship is with God.
a. True
b. False

9. As we _____ to worship, God _____ us to pass through everything.

10. Which realm is not a realm of Praise and Worship?
a. Praise in Spiritual Warfare
b. Realm of Dreams
c. Soulish Realm
d. Realm of Worship

11. When singing, how would we make sure we are not a distraction?
a. Practice before you play.
b. Make sure engineer has equipment ready before you start.
c. Don't allow practice during worship.
d. All the above

12. Which is not a guideline that will accompany what God is doing?

a. Realize we are created to praise God.

b. Come before Him with a pure heart.

c. Play with confidence in yourself as a great musician

d. Come desiring God to move.

e. As God moves flow with Him.

13. Our responsibility is to _____ God not to _____ God to _____ us.

14. If the congregation is not singing with us, what should we not do?

a. Focus on God

b. Yell at the congregation

c. Play songs that the congregation may know

d. Make sure that the songs are not too high or too low.

DEVO DAY 4:

PRAISE AND WORSHIP

We learned 'Who is God' in the first chapter of the series 'Journey to the Rock'. We also learned that Jesus is a being who has feelings, who has thoughts about us. And we learned that a life in Christ is a relationship we develop with Him.

One way we can develop this relationship is by praise and worship. Praise and worship are powerful tools in the "toolbox" we receive after we surrender our lives to Jesus. We can use these tools to express our love and honor Him, to encourage our Spirit, aid in our spiritual battles, and so much more.

SO, WHAT IS PRAISE AND WORSHIP AND HOW DO WE DO IT?

Praise and Worship: What It Isn't

Whether we have the talent to sing or not, we are called to praise and worship Him! We don't have to be on our church's or youth group's worship team to use this incredible gift. We just must have the right heart.

Back before we gave our lives to Jesus, how many of us remember using music as a way to get ourselves to "feel" a certain way? Perhaps we woke up feeling not ok or "off", so we would find music to help us "get happy" if we weren't. Or maybe we did wake up happy, so we would turn on music that helped us express our joy. This kind of manipulation is a habit that can creep into our worship life, if we're not careful.

Praise and worship is not for showing off our talent or skill. Nor is it to point out someone else's "lack" of skill or talent. It's not to manipulate God into giving us something, or getting us somewhere.

Praise and Worship: What It Is

The Bible says:

> *"Make a joyful noise to the Lord, all the earth;*
> *break forth and sing for joy, yes, sing praises!*
> *"*

PSALM 98:4 AMPC

"Break forth and sing for joy"!

We are called to praise Jesus in every and any circumstances – when we're happy, sad, under stress, in trouble, in fear.

And it doesn't always have to be the latest worship song either! We can make our own songs to Him and for Him!

The biggest reason for worship is that it ministers to Jesus. When we think of the word "minister" maybe we think of a person in a church. But one of the older definitions of minister is actually a verb. It means to attend to someone's needs. Does God need anything? No. But isn't it an amazing thing that we can attend to His heart in worship? That somehow, we in our smallness, can actually do something that pleases Him, that shows Him affection, love and brings Him glory and honor?

Another reason we worship is speaking His truth over our circumstances, our emotions and our lives! Just as God spoke the whole word into existence ("Let there be..."), our verbal worship and praise to Him expresses who He is. And He uses that audible declaration to help us gain our breakthrough! He uses our offering of praise and worship to bring us joy, strength, comfort, wisdom. There is so much God does by His Spirit, when we sing out His Truth!

Even if God doesn't choose to change our situations, praise and worship always changes US!

ANOINTING: THE DIVIDING FACTOR

The power behind worship isn't because we are wanting something to happen, and it's not something we "work up". The power comes from Who we're singing to.

The intention of our heart is key.

Singing a song just to sing it, won't minister to Him, and has no power to transform us or our situations. There's a something more that's needed, and it comes from God, and that's His anointing. Maybe you've heard of the word anointing in church. It can mean to put oil on and bless someone, but in this sense, it means when God's presence comes on us by His Spirit and gives us the power and ability to do things we ourselves could not do alone. He's altogether perfect, so who better to know how to worship Him, than Him!

When His anointing is on us, it creates a partnership or synergy between us, the Holy Spirit, Jesus and God that has an effect far greater than what we could do alone. And when He comes and anoints us, it's His own hand working through us, to do the impossible.

PRAISE AND WORSHIP ARE SO MUCH MORE.

Praise and worship are so much more than just a song with instruments. It is how we live, how we serve God in our daily lives. Our firm decision to not sin against Him, to keep our hearts and lives pure before Him, is worship as well!

When we're feeling good and thankful, worship and praise is a breeze! It's easy to sing about how good He is when we're on the mountain top.

But there is a power and depth to worship we learn in times where it's not so easy or convenient. When we are gripped with grief, fear, pain, turmoil, uncertainty, sickness — can we still purposefully choose to pour out our worship to

God? This kind of worship can feel and be costly to us – but He sees it as a most precious gift. And it's a gift that we have the privilege of bringing to Him.

> "O nations of the world, recognize the Lord,
>   recognize that the Lord is glorious and strong.
>   Give to the Lord the glory he deserves! Bring
>   your offering and come into his presence.
>   Worship the Lord in all his holy splendor. Let
>   all the earth tremble before him. The world
>   stands firm and cannot be shaken."

1 CHRONICLES 16:28-30 NLT

Reflect and Respond:

- What are some things you learned about worship in today's reading that you didn't know before?
- What do you feel the Lord showing you about your own praise and worship?
- How will you apply what you've read to your own relationship with Jesus?

Write a prayer to the Lord about what you've read today, and how it touched your heart:

Journal

_____
_____
_____
_____
_____
_____
_____
_____
_____
_____
_____
_____
_____
_____
_____
_____
_____
_____
_____

Think outside the box

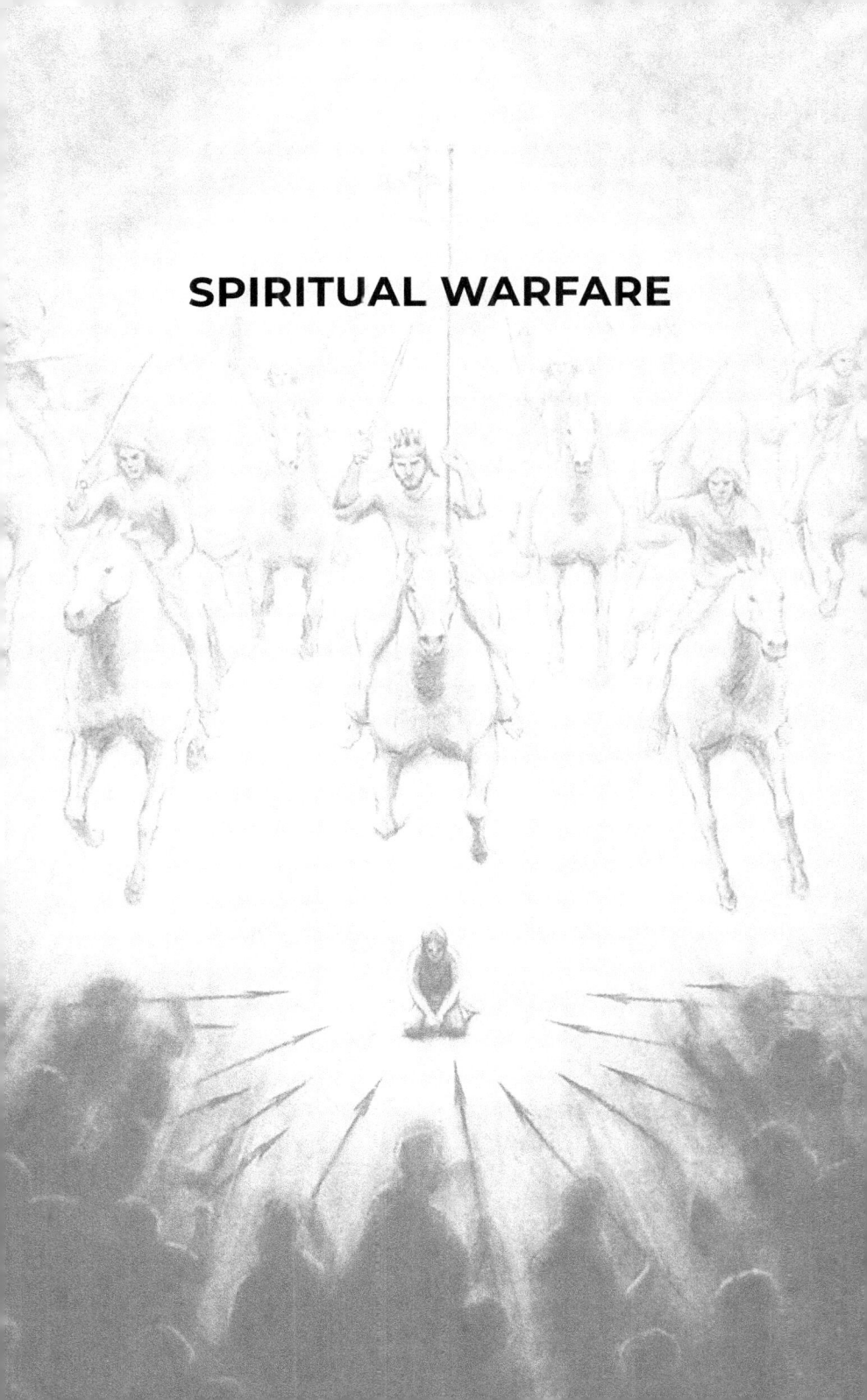

SPIRITUAL WARFARE

SPIRITUAL WARFARE

Spiritual Warfare always sounds like something that we do. But it is God doing it through us, if God is not doing it, we should not be either. God wants His people free more than we do. God sent His son Jesus to set the captives free.

During this study look to Him for His divine guidance – who He wants to help and His compassion for the broken. Remember we only want to do what you see God doing. Also, it is good that we do not try to do Spiritual Warfare alone, have someone with you who is a seasoned warrior.

The Battle is not ours; **it is God's.**

THE CAPTAIN OF THE HOST

And it came to pass, when Joshua was by Jericho,
that he lifted his eyes and looked, and behold,
a Man stood opposite him with His sword
drawn in His hand. And Joshua went to Him

and said to Him, "Are You for us or for our
adversaries?"
So He said, "No, but as Commander of the army
of the Lord I have now come."
And Joshua fell on his face to the earth and
worshiped, and said to Him, "What does my
Lord say to His servant?" Then the
Commander of the Lord's army said to
Joshua, "Take your sandal off your foot, for
the place where you stand is holy." And
Joshua did so

JOSHUA 5:13-15

God is not for us – we are for Him. In our daily lives look for the changes that God is interested in making. It is not how we want to change our friend or our spouse. When we are faced with a serious need for Spiritual Warfare, we remember that God loves that person more than we can – so much He sent His Son to die and live for them. We must allow God to fight the battle.

3 KEYS TO SPIRITUAL WARFARE:

Not by Might not by power but by His Spirit

"This is the word of the Lord to Zerubbabel: 'Not
by might nor by power, but by My Spirit,'
Says the Lord of hosts.

ZECHARIAH 4:6

Jesus did the thing He saw His Father do:

> *Then answered Jesus and said unto them, Verily,*
> *verily, I say unto you, The Son can do*
> *nothing of himself, but what he sees the*
> *Father do: for whatsoever things he does,*
> *these also does the Son likewise.*

JOHN 5:19

The blood of Jesus – paid it all.

One of the most drastic films of the battle that Jesus fought can be seen in the movie *Passion of Christ*. In all of the visual horror displayed; we see Christ flogged, beaten and hung on the cross, we must realize that the horror Jesus actually experienced was greater than could be shown through a movie.

Jesus paid the price to carry the authority over the devil. We may only walk in His authority.

LET'S REVIEW - THE CAPTAIN OF THE HOST

THE WARRIOR

God allows circumstances in our lives. They are not to destroy us, but to teach us and strengthen us.

Teach my hands to war

*He teaches my hands to make war, So that my
    arms can bend a bow of bronze.*
*You have also given me the shield of Your
    salvation; Your right hand has held me up,
    Your gentleness has made me great.*
*You enlarged my path under me, So my feet did
    not slip.*
*I have pursued my enemies and overtaken them;
    Neither did I turn back again till they were
    destroyed.*
*I have wounded them, So that they could not rise;
    They have fallen under my feet.*
*For You have armed me with strength for the
    battle; You have subdued under me those who
    rose up against me. You have also given me
    the necks of my enemies, So that I destroyed
    those who hated me.*

PSALMS 18:34-40

See also 2 Samuel 22:35.

A Psalm of David.

> *1 Blessed be the LORD my strength, which
>   **teacheth my hands to war, and my fingers to
>   fight:** 2 My goodness, and my fortress; my
>   high tower, and my deliverer; my shield, and
>   he in whom I trust; who subdueth my people
>   under me.*

PSALM 144:1, 2

For the weapons of our warfare are not [a]carnal
but mighty in God for pulling down
strongholds,

2 CORINTHIANS 10:4

People have said to me that they physically put on the armor of God every day. I tell them, "I never take it off." Nighttime is a struggle for many people. The armor of God is the same as putting on the Lord Jesus Christ. You put Jesus on and never take Him off. There are specific times that we refer to that armor – and recognize its use. We make sure our minds are protected and that we do not open doors through lying or other sins.

Armor of God

> "*10 Finally, my brethren, be strong in the Lord,*
> *and in the power of his might. 11 Put on the*
> *whole armour of God, that ye may be able to*
> *stand against the wiles of the devil. 12 For we*
> *wrestle not against flesh and blood, but*
> *against principalities, against powers, against*
> *the rulers of the darkness of this world,*
> *against spiritual wickedness in high places. 13*
> *Wherefore take unto you the whole armour*
> *of God, that ye may be able to withstand in*
> *the evil day, and having done all, to stand. 14*
> *Stand therefore, having your loins girt about*
> *with truth, and having on the breastplate of*
> *righteousness; 15 And your feet shod with the*
> *preparation of the gospel of peace; 16 Above*

all, taking the shield of faith, wherewith ye
shall be able to quench all the fiery darts of
the wicked. 17 And take the helmet of
salvation, and the sword of the Spirit, which
is the word of God: 18 Praying always with
all prayer and supplication in the Spirit, and
watching thereunto with all perseverance
and supplication for all saints;"

EPHESIANS 6:10-18

The battle is the Lord's – it is not ours.

If you went to an army base and used their weapons – it does not necessarily mean you are in the army. If you are in the army the first thing you declare is your allegiance to that country, government and officers who train and lead you. Just because people "prophesy, cast out devils and do wonderful works" does not mean that they are doing what God is showing them to do. It does not mean that they are being moved with compassion or in obedience to the King of Kings.

"Cast out Devils" – I never knew you.

Not every one that saith unto me, Lord, Lord,
shall enter into the kingdom of heaven; but he
that doeth the will of my Father which is in
heaven. 22 Many will say to me in that day,
Lord, Lord, have we not prophesied in thy
name? and in thy name have cast out devils?
and in thy name done many wonderful

works? 23 And then will I profess unto them,
I never knew you: depart from me, ye that
work iniquity.

MATTHEW 7:21-23

God is training warriors for His Kingdom who will know who He is; follow His direction and who move with His Love. Then, when we meet Him, He will say welcome home my faithful servant.

Read: II Chronicles 20

Jehoshaphat had a serious problem. The enemy was going to destroy his kingdom. Three armies – if you please, were headed his way with one idea in mind. Destruction! Let's see what steps Jehoshaphat took.

Jehoshaphat claimed a fast and sought the Lord

> *1 It came to pass after this also, [that] the*
> *children of Moab, and the children of*
> *Ammon, and with them [other] beside the*
> *Ammonites, came against Jehoshaphat to*
> *battle. 2 Then there came some that told*
> *Jehoshaphat, saying, There cometh a great*
> *multitude against thee from beyond the sea*
> *on this side Syria; and, behold, they [be] in*
> *Hazazontamar, which [is] Engedi. 3 And*
> *Jehoshaphat feared, and set himself to seek*
> *the LORD, and proclaimed a fast throughout*
> *all Judah. 4 And Judah gathered themselves*
> *together, to ask [help] of the LORD: even out*

*of all the cities of Judah they came to seek the
LORD.*

II CHRONICLES 20:1-4

God's answer to Jehoshaphat

*And he said, Hearken ye, all Judah, and ye
inhabitants of Jerusalem, and thou king
Jehoshaphat, Thus saith the LORD unto you,
Be not afraid nor dismayed by reason of this
great multitude; for the battle [is] not yours,
but God's.*

2 CHRONICLES 20:15

When God answered Jehoshaphat, he worshipped Him.

*And Jehoshaphat bowed his head with [his] face
to the ground: and all Judah and the
inhabitants of Jerusalem fell before the
LORD, worshipping the LORD. 19 And the
Levites, of the children of the Kohathites, and
of the children of the Korhites, stood up to
praise the LORD God of Israel with a loud
voice on high.*

2 CHRONICLES 20:18, 19

Jehoshaphat rose early in the morning and obeyed God

*And they rose early in the morning, and went
forth into the wilderness of Tekoa:*

2 CHRONICLES 20:20

**Jehoshaphat set singers and dancers in the front to
praise God**

> *And when he had consulted with the people, he
> appointed singers unto the LORD, and that
> should praise the beauty of holiness, as they
> went out before the army, and to say, Praise
> the LORD; for his mercy [endureth] for ever. 22
> And when they began to sing and to praise, the
> LORD set ambushments against the children
> of Ammon, Moab, and mount Seir, which were
> come against Judah; and they were smitten.*

2 CHRONICLES 20:15

Jehoshaphat collected the spoil.

> *And when Jehoshaphat and his people came to
> take away the spoil of them, they found
> among them in abundance both riches with
> the dead bodies, and precious jewels, which
> they stripped off for themselves, more than
> they could carry away: and they were three
> days in gathering of the spoil, it was so much.*

2 CHRONICLES 20:25

Jehoshaphat took special care to thank God for His intervention.

> *And on the fourth day they assembled themselves in the valley of Berachah; for there they blessed the LORD: therefore the name of the same place was called, The valley of Berachah, unto this day. Then they returned, every man of Judah and Jerusalem, and Jehoshaphat in the forefront of them, to go again to Jerusalem with joy; for the LORD had made them to rejoice over their enemies. And they came to Jerusalem with psalteries and harps and trumpets unto the house of the LORD. And the fear of God was on all the kingdoms of [those] countries, when they had heard that the LORD fought against the enemies of Israel.*

2 CHRONICLES 20:26-29

God's presence – your refuge – your Key

More Keys:

- You cannot impart what you don't have.
- If God has not given you direction – do not move in presumption.
- No Fear – do not give place to fear.
- Do not focus on the enemy.

Focus on what is God doing and saying – right now. What is this person's greatest need? "God how should we pray in this circumstance? What is your direction?" Do not give place to worry and fear. Search the Word of God to know what His word says about the situation.

Although we are seeking and waiting upon God for His direction it does not mean that we do nothing – if you need a job, get up early in the morning and pray, clean yourself up and go look for a job. In the military the soldier prepares his weapons and waits for his orders. Do what you know you should do and also wait upon God.

Warfare in music – What did Jehoshaphat do?

Praise and worship is an important key. God inhabits the praises of His people and when we are ministering to someone or battling for our own lives we need His presence. Praise ministers to God and ministers to us as well.

Go 2 x 2

When praying deliverance for someone, counseling, or ministering to them – take someone with you. If you get into the position where you must minister or counsel someone of the opposite sex keep your heart before God and take someone with you. Do not become so emotionally involved with them that you miss helping them. It is best that men minister to men and women to women.

> *And he called [unto him] the twelve, and began to send them forth by two and two; and gave them power over unclean spirits*

Don't cast out in Anger, Arrogance or Pride

You cannot cast out sin with sin. Anger, Arrogance and Pride is sin.

Just because it irritates you does not mean it is a spirit or that it bothers God.

I have heard of people saying "I bind you in the name of Jesus" as they are speaking to their spouse or friend because that person is not doing what they want. This is not about us! It is about the Love of God being demonstrated to the world, so that they may know Him! Are we praying and fasting for our own selfish needs or for their salvation?

Guard your heart

People's emotions are so high during these times, we must keep focused that this is not about us, it is about **God's pure love being demonstrated** to this person, that they may be healed and restored to wholeness.

> *Keep thy heart with all diligence; for out of it*
> *[are] the issues of life.*

PROVERBS 4:23

> *Wherefore let him that thinketh he standeth take*
> *heed lest he fall.*

I CORINTHIANS 10:12

A bird may fly over but don't let them nest on your head.

Thoughts, thoughts, thoughts... Once we are free and as well as when we are working with others, a thought that comes to your mind does not mean that it is "the devil" or that we are defeated. When wrong thoughts come, **do not take them and dwell on them.** Neither do we need to condemn ourselves because a thought came into our mind. He will change our lives and our minds as we seek Him and let Him.

> *Then will I sprinkle clean water upon you, and ye shall be clean: from all your filthiness, and from all your idols, will I cleanse you.*

EZEKIEL 36:25

> *That he might sanctify and cleanse it with the washing of water by the word, That he might present it to himself a glorious church, not having spot, or wrinkle, or any such thing; but that it should be holy and without blemish.*

EPHESIANS 5:26-27

THE WARRIOR

Armor of Christ

> *Therefore take up the whole armor of God, that you may be able to withstand in the evil day, and having done all, to stand. Stand therefore, having girded your waist with truth, having put on the breastplate of righteousness, and having shod your feet with the preparation of the gospel of peace; above all, taking the shield of faith with which you will be able to quench all the fiery darts of the wicked one. And take the helmet of salvation, and the sword of the Spirit, which is the word of God; praying always with all prayer and supplication in the Spirit, being watchful to this end with all perseverance and supplication for all the saints—*

> EPHESIANS 6:13-18

> *But put on the Lord Jesus Christ, and make no provision for the flesh, to fulfill its lusts.*

> ROMANS 13:14

Notice how the Armor of Christ is covered when **we put on the Lord Jesus Christ?** Our head is covered with His

Salvation, Water Baptism destroys the Adamic Nature. When we walk in His Spirit we cover our most life giving areas with Truth and Righteousness?

When we put on the Lord Jesus Christ and make no provision for the flesh – we live with His Armor.

The enemy hates God. He hates us because we were formed in God's image, and we remind him of God. We do not trust the enemy or what he says. When we see him we ask "Lord what do You want me to do about this situation." We begin praying for the person and seeking God for the person's salvation. Then when it is time to pray, we bind those powers to the pit of hell in the name of Jesus Christ. We pray by the authority of the One who paid the price.

EXCERPT FROM "INTERCESSION"

Read Daniel Chapter 10.

Daniel started to pray, and God heard it from the moment he set His heart toward God. He heard and knew the cry of Daniel's heart. But the powers, the principalities in the air that stood prevented that prayer from coming through to God. And the whole thing as Daniel was praying the Lord was revealing himself to Daniel. It was Christ that Daniel saw and that ministered to him. But he said that it took that long 21 days to break through the principalities and powers that were in the air and Daniel knew that God heard his prayer, but he couldn't bring the answer back until he did the spiritual warfare in the heavens.

I know the powers of Satan are heavier over some cities than others. These are powers that the enemy has set over areas to linger there. So Daniel didn't eat. I think he must have fasted those 21 days. But the Lord wanted him to know that the moment he set his heart to pray – God heard his prayer.

I know this is true. God has given us such a mighty thing and we are blessed with the Holy Ghost as well. We're blessed with One that takes that prayer and takes it to the Father according to the will of God. We're blessed today even though the principalities were cast down to the earth. Now, Satan can't go into the heavens to declare things against us to the Father. God has given us authority and dominion to pull down the powers and principalities through prayer and intercession.

REV. AGNES I. NUMER

THE ENEMY

Jesus I know, Paul I know, but who are you?

> *And the evil spirit answered and said, Jesus I know, and Paul I know; but who are ye?*

ACTS 19:15

God's enemy is strong and powerful; he is not to be played with.

> *How art thou fallen from heaven, O Lucifer, son*

of the morning! [how] art thou cut down to
the ground, which didst weaken the nations!

ISAIAH 14:12

The enemy hates God. He hates us because we were formed in God's image, and we remind him of God.

> *And the LORD God said unto the serpent,*
> *Because thou hast done this, thou [art] cursed*
> *above all cattle, and above every beast of the*
> *field; upon thy belly shalt thou go, and dust*
> *shalt thou eat all the days of thy life: 15 And I*
> *will put enmity between thee and the*
> *woman, and between thy seed and her seed;*
> *it shall bruise thy head, and thou shalt bruise*
> *his heel.*

GENESIS 3:14, 15

Carnal Nature: Everything we were before Christ, everything we inherited from Adam, everything that functions on the DNA of Adam.

Our carnal nature – no matter how we dress it or disguise it has no power when it comes to spiritual things. And it has no power over God's enemy. Our Hope and Strength is:

Jesus paid the price to carry the authority over the devil.

We tap into and walk in His authority.

> *For though we walk in the flesh, we do not war*

according to the flesh. For the weapons of our
warfare are not carnal but mighty in God for
pulling down strongholds, casting down
arguments and every high thing that exalts
itself against the knowledge of God, bringing
every thought into captivity to the obedience
of Christ,

II CORINTHIANS 10:3-5

Don't give place to the devil

Spiritual Warfare is carried out through the authority of
Jesus Christ. We cannot cast out sin with sin. This scripture
tells us how not to give place to the devil:

> *That you put off, concerning your former*
> *conduct, the old man which grows corrupt*
> *according to the deceitful lusts, and be*
> *renewed in the spirit of your mind, and that*
> *you put on the new man which was created*
> *according to God, in true righteousness and*
> *holiness.*
> *Therefore, putting away lying, "Let each one of*
> *you speak truth with his neighbor," for we*
> *are members of one another. "Be angry, and*
> *do not sin": do not let the sun go down on*
> *your wrath, nor give [a]place to the devil. Let*
> *him who stole steal no longer, but rather let*
> *him labor, working with his hands what is*
> *good, that he may have something to give*
> *him who has need. Let no corrupt word*

proceed out of your mouth, but what is good
for necessary edification, that it may impart
grace to the hearers. And do not grieve the
Holy Spirit of God, by whom you were sealed
for the day of redemption. Let all bitterness,
wrath, anger, [c]clamor, and evil speaking be
put away from you, with all malice. And be
kind to one another, tenderhearted, forgiving
one another, even as God in Christ forgave
you.

EPHESIANS 4:22-32

The Enemy's weapon of division:

When we train ministers and Pastors overseas one of the first questions that comes up was why was it that when they went on the Mission field to a dark place, they always ended up fighting with each other. God commands a blessing when there is unity. God's enemy enjoys division – one of the greatest war tactics is to cause division in the enemy's camp – cause them to fight amongst themselves.

When we feel this presence of Division pray against it and **allow God's love to flow** through us for each other and refuse to react to flesh with our flesh.

THE CAPTIVE

THE CAPTIVE

The Captive in this section can be any person, your neighbor, the person on the street, your family; even you can be a captive.

God never intended for us to be captives.

> *But unto every one of us is given grace according to the measure of the gift of Christ. 8 Wherefore he saith, When he ascended up on high, he led captivity captive, and gave gifts unto men*

> EPHESIANS 4:7, 8

> *The Spirit of the Lord [is] upon me, because he hath anointed me to preach the gospel to the poor; he hath sent me to heal the*

brokenhearted, to preach deliverance to the
captives, and recovering of sight to the blind,
to set at liberty them that are bruised, To
preach the acceptable year of the Lord.

LUKE 4:18, 19

From before the fall of the first Adam, God had a plan to restore His people back to Himself.

God's Heart is continually moved with compassion for His people that they may truly embrace His nature, His character – and live with His peace.

LORD, thou wilt ordain peace for us: for thou
also hast wrought all our works in us. O
LORD our God, [other] lords beside thee have
had dominion over us: [but] by thee only will
we make mention of thy name. [They are]
dead, they shall not live; [they are] deceased,
they shall not rise: therefore hast thou visited
and destroyed them, and made all their
memory to perish.

ISAIAH 26:12-14

In our lives God does not just want to destroy the enemy but to cause even the enemy's memory to perish! This is God's plan! Many captives do not realize God wants them to have peace.

Jesus cast out a devil that was mute... the person could not speak. When He was finished people wondered how this could be. Imagine the fear and bewilderment – this deliverance was something no one had ever seen during Jesus' day. And then, Jesus took that opportunity to teach a lesson on spiritual warfare to those that had an ear to hear:

> *"When an unclean spirit goes out of a man, he goes through dry places, seeking rest; and finding none, he says, 'I will return to my house from which I came.' And when he comes, he finds it swept and put in order. Then he goes and takes with him seven other spirits more wicked than himself, and they enter and dwell there; and the last state of that man is worse than the first."*

LUKE 11:24-26

"Jesus didn't go through the crucifixion just to do a halfway job. He did a perfect work – it's we that do a halfway job.

God gave me a vision of a mansion. It was a beautiful mansion, but it was filthy. He said this is the way you were. He said I bought you but now I'm going to clean you up. You are like this mansion: cobwebs, black walls, filth all over the place and then the Lord said I'm going to rejuvenate you and I'm going to change you.

We say I love you God, and I will let you clean my house –
but the other rooms are locked! That's the way we want to
serve the Lord but that isn't the way we should serve the
Lord. We either have to open the whole house to Him or He
won't take any of it.

What if you bought a house and the former owner wants to
live in that house – you pay for a whole house, and he keeps
3/4th of it?

It's the same way with Jesus – we can't halfway serve Him.
We have to come with all our heart, with all our soul, mind,
and strength – body, mind and soul. Jesus paid that price.

God delivers someone and their "house" is swept clean.
How do they fill their "house?"

> *Then he goes and takes with* him *seven other
> spirits more wicked than himself, and they
> enter and dwell there; and the last* state *of
> that man is worse than the first."*

LUKE 11:26

After deliverance people can feel empty and a bit lost. The
former lord of that area in their life is gone and now what
do they do? These areas need to be filled with God! Pray for
God to fill the person with His Peace and His Joy. If they are
not born again, teach them about Salvation and ask them if
they would ask Jesus into their heart. Lead them to the next
level in their walk with God. Teach them how to close doors

that they opened to the enemy. Encourage them to go to church and fellowship with those who will minister strength and healing to them.

> *When Jesus had raised Himself up and saw no one but the woman, He said to her, "Woman, where are those accusers of yours? Has no one condemned you?" She said, "No one, Lord." And Jesus said to her, "Neither do I condemn you; go and sin no more."*

> JOHN 8:10, 11

NO LONGER THE CAPTIVE

OUR WEAPONS

> *For though we walk in the flesh, we do not war according to the flesh. For the weapons of our warfare are not carnal but mighty in God for pulling down strongholds, casting down arguments and every high thing that exalts itself against the knowledge of God, bringing every thought into captivity to the obedience of Christ, and being ready to punish all disobedience when your obedience is fulfilled.*

> II CORINTHIANS 10:3-6

Whose report will you believe?

The Word of God says that we shall know the truth and the truth will set us free. Where does the Truth come from? Will you believe the Word of God or will you believe your horoscope or someone who reads your palm. Will you believe the creation — or the Creator? Will you cleave to God's Divine character or Adam's character?

We cannot vacillate back and forth, either the battle is the Lord's, or we will fight with our carnal mind – our earthly knowledge, with the Adamic DNA. We cannot be double minded and expect to remain free.

Renounce the bondage

Pray for the blindness to come off the mind of the captive so that He may see Jesus, the Author and Finisher of his faith. The Captive must reach out to God, we can do part of the warfare, but the captive must make his own decisions so that he will remain free.

What does renounce mean?

Renounce means to **"disown."** Whatever chain the captive has, he must let it go and "disown" it. Repent of it and Walk away from it. One day Jesus showed me a field with a "No Trespassing" sign on it. When we belong to Jesus the devil is a trespasser. Tell him. We must let go of all of the lies, dishonesty, craftiness and sins that open the door for "the Trespasser." Once we belong to God, we have the right to tell the "the Trespasser" to get off and never come back.

What did Jesus do?

What did Jesus do when He was confronted with Spiritual Warfare?

After Jesus was in the wilderness and conquered Satan by not giving into temptation, He went into the Temple with a testimony, and with a declaration of His purpose in life.

Read from Luke 4:

> Then Jesus, being filled with the Holy Spirit, returned from the Jordan and was led by the Spirit into the wilderness, being tempted for forty days by the devil. And in those days He ate nothing, and afterward, when they had ended, He was hungry. And the devil said to Him, "If You are the Son of God, command this stone to become bread." But Jesus answered him, saying, "It is written, 'Man shall not live by bread alone, but by every word of God.'" Then the devil, taking Him up on a high mountain, showed Him all the kingdoms of the world in a moment of time. And the devil said to Him, "All this authority I will give You, and their glory; for this has been delivered to me, and I give it to whomever I wish.Therefore, if You will worship before me, all will be Yours." And Jesus answered and said to him, "Get behind Me, Satan! For it is written, 'You shall worship the Lord your God, and Him only you shall serve.'" Then he brought Him to Jerusalem, set Him on the pinnacle of the temple, and said to Him, "If You are the Son of God, throw Yourself down from here. For it is written: 'He shall give His angels charge

over you, To keep you,' "and, 'In their hands
they shall bear you up, Lest you dash your
foot against a stone.' " And Jesus answered
and said to him, "It has been said, 'You shall
not tempt the Lord your God.' " Now when
the devil had ended every temptation, he
departed from Him until an opportune time.
Then Jesus returned in the power of the Spirit
to Galilee, and news of Him went out
through all the surrounding region.

LUKE 4:1-14

The Spirit of the Lord [is] upon me, because he
hath anointed me to preach the gospel to the
poor; he hath sent me to heal the
brokenhearted, to preach deliverance to the
captives, and recovering of sight to the blind,
to set at liberty them that are bruised, To
preach the acceptable year of the Lord.

LUKE 4:18, 19

This is the purpose of Jesus coming to the earth! That He
might set us free! It is what God wants for us that we may be
brought back to the Father. Oh, if Adam and Eve had not
chosen to listen to the Devil! Oh, that we would realize all
that God has for us and stop listening to those created
beings but listen to the Creator of the Universe. How free we
would be! What a powerful perspective from the One who
sees ALL of the past, the present, the future and the

eternity... You must make up your mind – Life or Death, Freedom or Bondage, Good or Evil. We cannot have both.

> *And I heard a loud voice saying in heaven, Now is come salvation, and strength, and the kingdom of our God, and the power of his Christ: for the accuser of our brethren is cast down, which accused them before our God day and night. And they overcame him by the blood of the Lamb, and by the word of their testimony; and they loved not their lives unto the death.*

REVELATIONS 12:10-11

OUR WEAPONS

Spiritual warfare is not a game, it is something that God does through us to help others know Him and become free. This gift from God to us is so that people do not have to spend the rest of their lives tormented and in captivity. Torment was not made for man, hell was not made for man – we must choose to be free to live eternally in His Love, His Peace and His Joy.

We must not agree with the enemy that inner torment is for us and that terrible things must always happen to us. In this world we have tribulation, but Jesus has overcome the world! God's eternal life began when we asked Jesus to be our Lord and Savior. That Eternal Kingdom began growing in our hearts. In this Kingdom we have Peace and Joy – no matter the circumstance.

When Jesus was drawn by the Spirit into the wilderness to be tempted of the devil, the greatest weapon Jesus had was that He knew God and that He knew God's Word. He used the Word of God against Satan and Jesus refused to do things against the Nature of God. As we know the Truth, that Truth sets us free.

Take time to know God, to know His Truth, to know His nature – to know Him. When the enemy of God and the enemy of our soul comes – hide in God's presence and obey His command.

The battle is the Lord's.

REVIEW: SPIRITUAL WARFARE

QUESTIONS FOR DISCUSSION

1. THE CAPTAIN OF THE HOST

When and how did Jesus:

- Prepare himself for Spiritual Warfare in Luke 4?
- Do Spiritual warfare?
- Cast out devils?

Where does the Bible mention that the Disciples and others – successfully and unsuccessfully cast out devils?

Explain what happened.

2. THE WARRIOR

- Define the war.
- What is the battle?
- What is our goal?

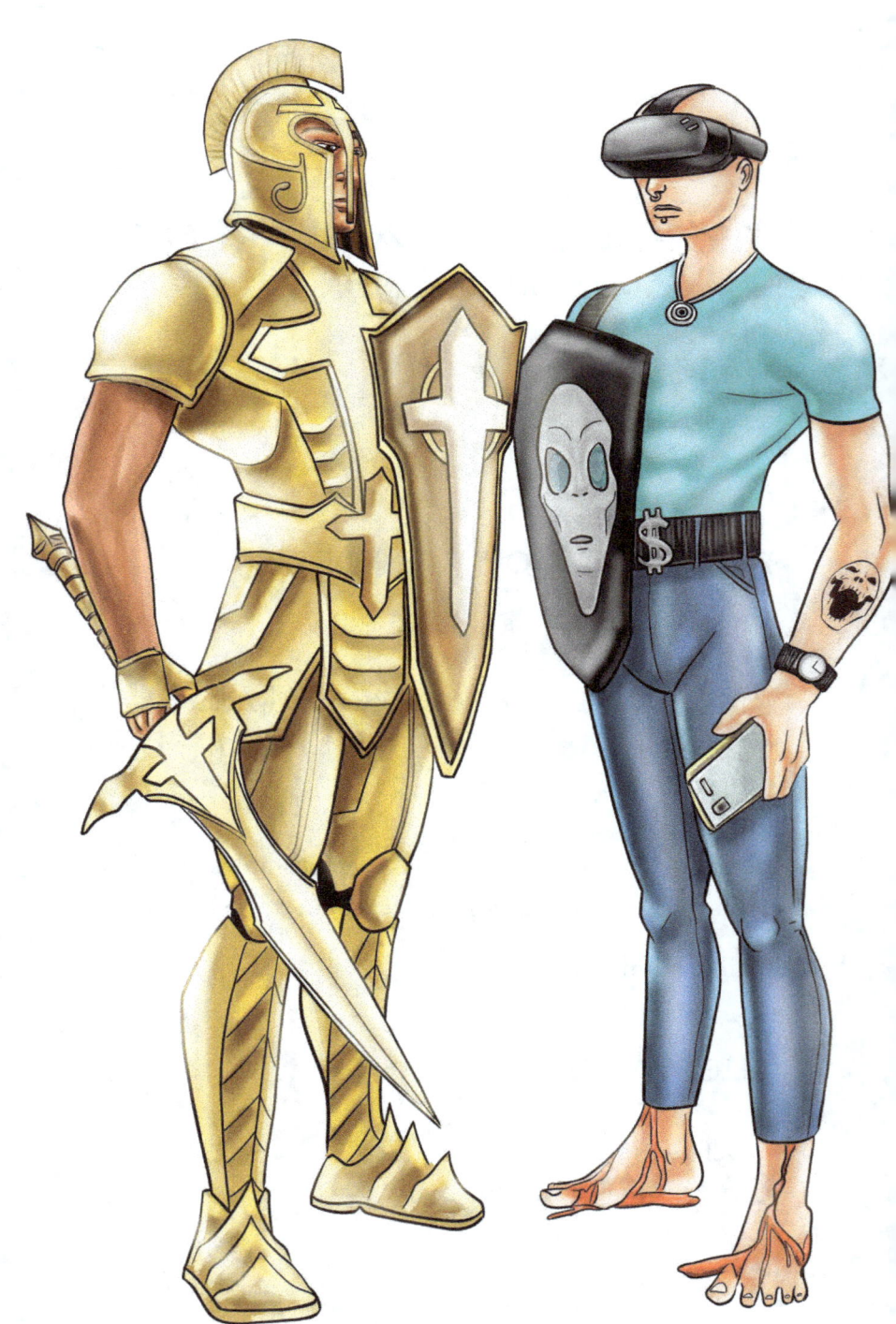

3. THE ENEMY

Critical Thinking Questions

Using the information covered in this session what do you think the answers would be?

If God's enemy had armor what would it look like?

The first one is filled in for you.

ARMOR CHRIST

Loins - Truth
Breastplate - Righteousness
Feet - Preparation of The Gospel of Peace
Shield - Faith
Helmet - Salvation
Sword of the Spirit - Word Of God

ARMOR ANTI-CHRIST

What is the parallel armor of the anti-Christ?

Loins - Deception
Breastplate -
Feet -
Shield -
Helmet -
Sword of the Spirit -

HOW MIGHT GOD'S ENEMY USE THE FOLLOWING KEYS TO HOLD SOMEONE CAPTIVE?

Condemnation
Presumption

4. THE CAPTIVE

Critical Thinking Questions

Using the information covered in this session, how would you answer these questions?

THE CAPTIVE'S CHAINS

There can be attitudes, addictions, different things that seem to control our lives where we are not free. Name five ways someone may have opened doors to God's enemy and may now be captive:

a)

b)

c)

d)

e)

GROUP DISCUSSION QUESTIONS

How do chains get reinforced?
Why are they there?
How will they not come back?
Why did Jesus say go and sin no more?

5. OUR WEAPONS

List five weapons from our Spiritual Warfare Session
a) God's Anointing
b)
c)
d)
e)

Critical Thinking Questions:

When you read the excerpt from "Don't Measure by Yourself" by Rev. Agnes I. Numer, what hope does that give you for spiritual warfare experiences you may encounter or what understanding did it give you from past experiences that you had with spiritual warfare?

QUIZ: SPIRITUAL WARFARE

1. Spiritual warfare is not something we do; it is something God does through us
a. True
b. False

2. Joshua's experience with the Captain of the Hosts teaches us that
a. We might encounter an angel at any time
b. God is not for us – we are for Him
c. The devil can appear as an angel of light

3. God allows difficult circumstances in our lives to strengthen us
a. True
b. False

4. People who "prophesy, cast out devils and do wonderful works" must be doing God's will

a. True

b. False

5. In spiritual warfare we must focus on the enemy

a. True

b. False

6. In spiritual warfare, God's Presence is your key. Select another key below

a. Do not move in presumption

b. Fully focus on what the enemy is doing

c. Keep yourself very busy

7. Focus on what is God doing and saying – right now and:

a. What is this person's greatest need?

b. "God how should we pray in this circumstance?"

c. "What is your direction?"

d. All of the above

8. We should condemn ourselves if an ungodly thought comes to us during warfare

a. True

b. False

9. Spiritual warfare is carried out by the authority of Jesus

a. True

b. False

10. In warfare, when you feel the presence of the spirit of division we should:

a. Pray against it

b. Allow God's love to flow for each other

c. Refuse to give place to it

d. All of the above

11. All of the armor of God is included when we put on Jesus

a. True

b. False

12. After experiencing deliverance, a person might feel empty

a. True

b. False

13. The spiritual weapons we have are mighty through God. They can

a. Pull down of strong holds

b. Cast down imaginations

c. Bring thoughts into captivity to obey Christ

d. All of the above

14. What does renounce mean?

a. To speak critically of someone

b. To disown, repent or walk away

c. An open invitation

15. Jesus conquered Satan by not giving into temptation

a. True

b. False

DEVO DAY 5:

THE CHRISTIAN HERO

Ever watched a wrestling match and find yourself throwing punches in the air... even though you are not the one in the ring?

Have you ever watched a football game and all you ever wanted to do was; to be given the chance to go in the game and score the winning goal?

What about wanting to take the driver seat from the driver?

The Bible calls our spiritual warfare the good fight of faith.

This fight is termed good because the winner is already known. Good will always overcome evil and righteousness will always overcome sin.

In our Christian journey we often confront many obstacles and challenges that may try to prevent us from living our lives in a way pleasing to God.

. . .

As Christians we must keep in mind that:

1. The battle is not ours, but Gods.
2. God is not for us; we are for him.
3. We must allow God to fight the battles with this mind in us, then we will overcome all the craftiness of the enemy.

Have you ever been in a spiritual warfare?

How did you overcome?

> *I returned and saw under the sun that — The race is not to the swift, Nor the battle to the strong, Nor bread to the wise, Nor riches to men of understanding, Nor favor to men of skill; But time and chance happen to them all.*

ECCLESIASTES 9:11

The scripture says that the race is not to the swift, neither is victory in spiritual warfare for the strong. Our victory over spiritual warfare is only possible when we put our trust in the blood of Jesus, and it's finished work by allowing his spirit to work in our lives and help us follow his footsteps everyday of our lives.

Sometimes we are puzzled and confused when we are faced with hard times; the Bible calls it the trial of our faith. This is necessary for our development as Christians. God allows circumstances in our lives not to destroy us, but to teach us, and equip us with His armor. Hence, anyone and everyone can face spiritual warfare, for, after we've been tried by fire, we will come out pure as gold. Psalm 66

I believe that God is intentional about equipping us, because he wants to raise spiritual warriors who would not just serve him but will know him personally and intentionally. It indeed is a rare privilege to be under God's tutelage and guidance. We are always safe in the hollow of His hands.

The Bible tells a story of King Jehoshaphat who was in spiritual warfare and didn't know what to do, he decided to seek his God's face, to listen to hear his voice, worship him and wait for His leading. Read 2 Chronicles 20.

Will you do same when faced with spiritual warfare?

Prerequisite to fight the good fight of faith:

1. Ensure you make God's presence, your refuge.
2. Do not cast out sin with sin.
3. Guard your heart diligently.
4. Ensure you do not fall for the enemy's weapon of division.
5. Renounce the bondage.

What other prerequisites do you think are necessary for fighting the good fight of faith?

MEMORY VERSE:

*Fight the good fight of faith, lay hold on eternal
life, to which you were also called and have*

confessed the good confession in the presence of many witnesses.

1 TIMOTHY 6:12

Prayer: Dear Lord, thank you for the privilege to be enlisted in your army, thank you because you have given me the victory through my Lord Jesus Christ. Help me to live a life pleasing before You and by Your Spirit overcome every spiritual warfare I may encounter. In Jesus Name. AMEN.

IMPACT OF ISAIAH 58

ISAIAH 58

Cry aloud, spare not, lift up thy voice like a
trumpet, and shew my people their
transgression, and the house of Jacob their
sins.

2 Yet they seek me daily, and delight to know my
ways, as a nation that did righteousness, and
forsook not the ordinance of their God: they
ask of me the ordinances of justice; they take
delight in approaching to God.

3 Wherefore have we fasted, say they, and thou
seest not? wherefore have we afflicted our
soul, and thou takest no knowledge? Behold,
in the day of your fast ye find pleasure, and
exact all your labours.

4 Behold, ye fast for strife and debate, and to
smite with the fist of wickedness: ye shall not
fast as ye do this day, to make your voice to
be heard on high.

5 *Is it such a fast that I have chosen? a day for a man to afflict his soul? is it to bow down his head as a bulrush, and to spread sackcloth and ashes under him? wilt thou call this a fast, and an acceptable day to the Lord?*

6 *Is not this the fast that I have chosen? to loose the bands of wickedness, to undo the heavy burdens, and to let the oppressed go free, and that ye break every yoke?*

7 *Is it not to deal thy bread to the hungry, and that thou bring the poor that are cast out to thy house? when thou seest the naked, that thou cover him; and that thou hide not thyself from thine own flesh?*

8 *Then shall thy light break forth as the morning, and thine health shall spring forth speedily: and thy righteousness shall go before thee; the glory of the Lord shall be thy reward.*

9 *Then shalt thou call, and the Lord shall answer; thou shalt cry, and he shall say, Here I am. If thou take away from the midst of thee the yoke, the putting forth of the finger, and speaking vanity;*

10 *And if thou draw out thy soul to the hungry, and satisfy the afflicted soul; then shall thy light rise in obscurity, and thy darkness be as the noon day:*

11 *And the Lord shall guide thee continually, and satisfy thy soul in drought, and make fat thy bones: and thou shalt be like a watered*

*garden, and like a spring of water, whose
waters fail not.*

*12 And they that shall be of thee shall build the
old waste places: thou shalt raise up the
foundations of many generations; and thou
shalt be called, The repairer of the breach,
The restorer of paths to dwell in.*

*13 If thou turn away thy foot from the sabbath,
from doing thy pleasure on my holy day; and
call the sabbath a delight, the holy of the
Lord, honourable; and shalt honour him, not
doing thine own ways, nor finding thine own
pleasure, nor speaking thine own words:*

*14 Then shalt thou delight thyself in the Lord;
and I will cause thee to ride upon the high
places of the earth, and feed thee with the
heritage of Jacob thy father: for the mouth of
the Lord hath spoken it.*

ISAIAH 58 KJV

ISAIAH 58 - THE VISION

In 1954, God gave Rev. Agnes I Numer a vision. It was a vision of Isaiah 58 and how God would demonstrate His love to the nations in these last days. The vision was given by the Spirit of Revelation. Since that time, the late Rev. Numer trained thousands of pastors and leaders globally in this amazing vision... **Demonstrating the Love of God to the Nations.**

THE VISION IN HER OWN WORDS

In 1954 , the Lord one day gave me the revelation of Isaiah, chapter 58. And it was so mighty, I was very aware that it was by the Spirit of Revelation.

I was washing dishes, it was Sunday morning, and I was asking the Lord a question. That question was if it was His will for us to buy a house in Sunland, Tujunga area. Now, we were living in that area, but God was beginning to speak to me about moving. He gave me a scripture, He said:

"Is it not yet a very little while, and Lebanon
shall be turned into a fruitful field, and the
fruitful field shall be esteemed as a forest?
Isaiah 29:17

I said, "Lord, but what does that have to do with what I asked you?"

He said, "Go and read... Isaiah 58."

As I dried my hands, and walked from my kitchen into the living room, and as I was walking through the room, all at once I was aware that something was happening to me. I was aware that my mind was just moved out of the way, I felt a vastness as big as all outdoors, and I was aware it was the Spirit of Revelation.

He began, as I opened Isaiah 58, to reveal to me the plan of the last days, and He showed it to me in minute detail, every phase of it, in the natural and in the spiritual. He showed me His plan to help the nations. He showed me how He was going to feed the hungry, clothe the naked, and meet the needs of the people. And that in this hour, which I believe is now, that He is going to move very quickly, by the flow of His Spirit. He is going to cause people to flow together, and do something that has never been done in the history of this world.

HE SHOWED ME MINISTRIES

He showed me ministries flowing together as one, with one not trying to outdo the other. He showed me warehouses filed with new clothing. He showed me something very wonderful, that it would not be used clothing, everything would be new. The equipment would not be old worn-out equipment, but it would be new. And that which He was going to do was to go into the nations, and He is going to show them how He would do it.

God is waiting for the nations of the earth to **acknowledge Him,** and when they acknowledge Him, He's going to pour out His blessings upon them. The devil is trying to prevent it, but I'm going to tell you this: In this day, **they are not going to stop Him.** This time it's not going to be defeated. He does it and man will not be able to say that they did it, because it will be so great that no man can claim the glory. God's going to receive the glory.

These things that He's going to do are mighty. The people that He has prepared are waiting. And when He speaks the word, they are going to move in their place, and God is going to perform it.

HE SHOWED HOW HE WOULD HELP THE NATIONS

He showed me how He was going to help the nations, to feed the hungry, to go in and teach the people themselves how to help the people. Missionaries have gone in, in the past, but for some reason the methods they've used has not caused the people to rise up and to learn for themselves. But God is going in with every provision, and as we teach the people in the natural and the spiritual, the spiritual and natural are going to flow together, and God is going to show them who He is. Now we have people all over the world who are trying to help, but God's plan is not going to fail. **He just needs the people who are trained by His Spirit to do it the way He wants it done.**

He also showed me the scientific things in the realm of the supernatural. And as things happen on the earth, **He is going to take care of His people, supply their needs and they will supply the needs of others.** We have had people ask us, "How do you do this?" We say, **"We don't do it, God does it all; all we do is flow by His Spirit."**

We watch the Lord join us with people who know how to move by the Spirit of the Lord, and we know that there is a job that is going to be done. God is going to do something in our lives as we obey Him. He said, "Our health would spring forth speedily and our light would be as the morning." But as we continue to move in obedience to the word of God and the Spirit of God, the light is going to get brighter and brighter. And then the Lord is going to say, "Here am I... what do you want? Here am I... what do you need?"

You see, as we move in obedience to the Lord, God will fulfill His promises. We've limited Him because we're afraid if we trust Him, He won't do it. Isn't that true? Too much to ask of the Lord.

He showed me the ships, and He gave me the word concerning them. He showed me transport planes, and then He showed me all the provision which He was going to give, that we would have training places all over the world, so that the people could be trained by the Spirit of the Lord. And so the Lord is doing exactly what He said, and we are seeing it come to pass. So that's why we're rejoicing, **because if God said it, He will do it ... and we can trust Him.**

THE IMPACT OF ISAIAH 58

THE FAST THAT GOD HAS NOT CHOSEN

We all have a tendency to think that the way we serve God is right, that it is very pleasing to the Lord. It is hard for us to hear anything different, especially when our way seems so right to us and so many people agree with us. This may be the hardest area of our life for us to hear; when we are doing a "good" thing that is not totally a God thing.

That is why Isaiah was told to:

> *Cry aloud, spare not, lift up thy voice like a trumpet, and show my people their transgression, and the house of Jacob their sins.*

ISAIAH 58:1

Isn't it very often true that we have to be shown something different in order to "see" where we are falling short? Let's look at where God's people in this chapter were missing it and see if this will help open our eyes to areas which are keeping us from having God's best. Let's take a minute to pray and open our hearts right now and ask God to help us, to be able to see.

The people in this chapter were seeking God daily, they were delighting to know His ways, they were asking God for right ways or laws, and they were delighting in coming near to Him (feeling His presence).

> *Yet they seek me daily, and delight to know my ways, as a nation that did righteousness, and forsook not the ordinance of their God: they ask of me the ordinances of justice; they take delight in approaching to God.*

ISAIAH 58:2

They couldn't understand why even though they were seeking and fasting and afflicting their souls that God was not responding.

> *Wherefore have we fasted, say they, and thou seest not? wherefore have we afflicted our soul, and thou takest no knowledge?*

ISAIAH 58:3

God sent Isaiah to declare like a trumpet to them where they were falling short of pleasing God.

WHAT ARE THESE THINGS THAT ISAIAH TRUMPETED?

In the day of your fast ye find pleasure.

- There is an "It's all about me" attitude we can get. Or worse yet, "look at me", or possibly, "what can I get spiritually out of this fasting" Seeking God is not all about us. It is most importantly all about Him and what is on His heart. Our Father God loves us. He wants to meet with us and share His Heart with us and how He loves the broken people who need Him.

You still exact all your labors

- Some versions say this means, "you drive hard your workers" this sounds like no generosity on the job, with the workers, without mercy or compassion in business. God desires to flow into every area of our lives including how we do business.

You fast for strife and debate

- Our flesh loves to be spiritual, and there can be a lot of competition among God's leaders. The word of God is very honest about the shortcomings and strengths of its "heroes of faith". Pride and competition in our lives can show up even in our fasting.

> *Where do wars and fights come from among*
> *you? Do they not come from your desires*
> *for pleasure that war in your members?*

JAMES 4:1

You fast to smite with the fist of wickedness

- If we don't love the people we are praying for we might not see things the way God does and we might not be praying according to His heart. This part is really not very pretty. These people were so determined they were right that they were willing to "fight for it"

> *...Ye shall not fast as ye do this day, to make your*
> *voice to be heard on high.*

ISAIAH 58:4

We can also be impressed with ourselves and our self-denial. But God is not impressed. Whatever is not done unto the Lord is sin. Jesus spoke against the practices of the Pharisees and Sadducees who loved religious rigors. (Read Matthew 23) There is something in our flesh that loves being religious but until we allow God to bring light into these dark areas He will not here us and we will still think that we are great.

God asked, "Are you still going to call this a fast, are you still going to go on thinking this is an acceptable day unto the Lord?"

> *Is it such a fast that I have chosen? a day for a*
> *man to afflict his soul? Is it to bow down his*
> *head as a bulrush, and to spread sackcloth*
> *and ashes under him? <u>Wilt thou call this a</u>*
> *<u>fast</u>, an acceptable day to the LORD?*
>
> ISAIAH 58:5

> *Ask all the people of the land and the priests,*
> *'When you fasted and mourned in the fifth*
> *and seventh months for the past seventy*
> *years, was it really for me that you fasted?*
>
> ZECHARIAH 7:5 NIV

Isaiah 58 is often referred to as the "fasting chapter" and people go on long fasts based on this chapter. This misses the real point God is making, that just denying ourselves food, water or other things might not be what will reach the ear of God. It might not be this kind of fasting that will make the deepest heart changes we are seeking for in our own selves. What moves the heart of our Father? How can we "be heard on high"?

THIS IS THE FAST THAT I HAVE CHOSEN – ISAIAH 58

There is another kind of self-denial that God makes very clear will be so pleasing to Him that He will hear our every whisper. **There is a fast that He has chosen!**

Break bands of wickedness

- If we live a fasted lifestyle, care about the freedom from spiritual bondages and addictions of others, than we care about ourselves; and allow God to flow through us, He will break those bands. It is uncomfortable, inconvenient and unfamiliar to us but as we push past all that is uncomfortable, we will find the Comforter supplying all of our needs and making up for all of our lacks.

Undo heavy burdens

- People carry many heavy things, sorrow, worry, guilt, poverty, debt, family concerns. God cares and He wants to care through us. When a family is going through a heavy situation, we can be there with the Love of God to lift the heaviness.

Let the oppressed go free

- Demonic oppression, whether fear, torment, suicide or violence, can be broken as we become God's representative. People came into our ministry both day and night with a serious need to be set free. No matter what day or what time, if the Spirit of the Lord was moving, we would move with Him, setting aside whatever else to minister to them. Many were set gloriously free. Each time we laid down our life for our "brethren" we also became more gloriously free.

Feed the hungry

- God cares, he provides, he wants to meet the needs of people who are hungry through us. Feeding the hungry is hard work, it is inconvenient; people will often be ungrateful; and not many people will notice us. It becomes a joy only when His love and Spirit are flowing through us. We have to set aside our flesh every day and take up God's anointing to touch needy people with His love, joy and grace. We may rebel, complain and make excuses, but as we press deeper into the flow of His Spirit we will find life; His resurrection life.
- God hears this kind of fasting.

Clothe the naked

- Did you notice the hole in his shoe; did you see the little girl look down because she knows her clothes are torn? Can you see what God sees? Can you imagine the love they would feel if someone gave them what they needed? If they gave it with a demonstration of kindness? Their lives would never be the same? Now that is fasting!

Bring outcast into your house

- One thing about the outcast is that nobody wants them... except for God. He died for them. Bringing these kinds of people into your house requires an extra grace that only comes when God asks you to do it. There are a lot of inconveniences, but when we choose to let God love others through us. How quickly we will change.

Caring for your own flesh

- We all know that sometimes the hardest people to love are our own family members. We can get so busy doing ministry or business that we overlook the ones closest to us. Can we minister the Love of God, and can we see the needs of those in our own home?
- God did not miss this important balance to our lives in this chapter. Being a good Mom or a great big brother can really require denying ourselves. A little sister can be such a bug and just when we were ready to relax. Go ahead, deny yourself and love on her. Many pastors and ministers miss this part and suffer the results later in life. God will anoint you to love your family. You will have many who adopt you also. We have many teachers, many leaders but so few "Fathers" and Mothers.

Meet the needs of hungry and afflicted souls

- Hungry souls don't need our sympathy, they need God's healing compassion, His loving kindness but they are often the most difficult people to love. They set up their walls of anger and rejection and will try to keep anyone from hurting them more. The very thing they need most is God's love. Will we seek God until we have the wisdom, authority and grace to reach them? Will we travail until they are healed? This is pouring out our own soul to meet their needs. **This is True Fasting.**
- Hungry souls can be demanding and draining. It seems like they can never get filled up. We can only give what God gives us. Let us seek God for the flow of His ministry through us. **People need Jesus through us.**

STOP making "yokes, putting forth the finger, and speaking vanity."

Yokes. Religious bondages that we wear and also put on other people.

> *For they bind heavy burdens and grievous to be borne, and lay them on men's shoulders; but they themselves will not move them with one of their fingers.*

> MATTHEW 23:4

- Isaiah 10:1; Luke 11:46; Acts 15:10; But all their works they do for to be seen of men:
- Teachings, practices and rules might lead men to believe how great we are but they don't lead people to Jesus. They are yokes and bondages. Jesus came to set men free. He came to fulfill the law through loving God not through rules.
- We need a heart change that only comes through an encounter with God. **STOP** living by rules that are not of God and forcing them on others.

Fingers. Pointing accusingly at others. Fault finding, dishonoring.

When we **STOP** finger pointing and begin interceding for God to move in people's lives He will hear us. We will then begin to live a life of honoring, encouraging, building up, nurturing, serving.

Vain words. Religious sounding "Bible talk."

What people really need is our transparency and God's compassion through us. **We do not have all the answers.** When we act like we have all the answers, we offend people and we offend God. God is the only answer and He will be the answer through us when we **STOP** vain words

Honor the Sabbath and delight in it by:

- Not speaking your own words. Delight to speak His words
- Not seeking your own pleasure. Delight to do His will

- Not finding your own ways. Delight to find His heart and know His ways

This is how Jesus lived.

> *So Jesus answered them, "I tell you the solemn truth, the Son can do nothing on his own initiative, **but only what he sees the Father doing.** For whatever the Father does, the Son does likewise.*

> JOHN 5:19

> *For I have not spoken of myself; but the Father which sent me, he gave me a commandment, what I should say, and what I should speak.*

> JOHN 12:49

> *For I have given unto them the words which thou gavest me.*

> JOHN 17:8

We might not mind doing God's will if we can do it our own way

There is a Sabbath rest that we can enter into. Hebrews 4 says that some must enter even though they did not enter in because of their grumbling and their unbelief. Do we trust Him when our ability is drained or do we complain? When things begin to look bad can we declare His word into the situation and just rest?

> *There remains, then, a Sabbath-rest for the*
> *people of God; for anyone who enters God's*
> *rest also rests from their works, just as God*
> *did from his.*

HEBREWS 4:9

There is a place in God where we are doing His works in His Strength. We begin to have a river flowing through us that also gives us rest even for our bodies, but first we must **STOP** our own laboring. God can train us if we ask Him.

NOW... WE BEGIN TO BUILD WITH GOD... BRINGING HIS KINGDOM TO EARTH

ISAIAH 58:12-14

Build the old waste places

- The enemy comes to steal, kill and destroy but Jesus came to give us life more abundantly. That abundant life in us begins to "make all things new". Places which have both spiritually and naturally been laid waste for generations will be built up through people filled with His Spirit and His Kingdom. He knows how to take waste places and make them a fruitful garden.

- We have experienced so many times when we went to an area in great need, and cleaned and repaired in the natural, that God brought freedom in the spiritual realms.

Raise up the foundations of many generations

- People, families and communities are broken to their very foundations. Usually there is a long history of traumatic events that have rent the fabric of their society. They often carry an identity of victims and not victors. These foundations of lives and communities can be raised up again through the people of God. They can again have a firm foundation and a new identity on which to build which is based on forgiveness, reconciliation and restoration.

Repair the breaches

- Breaches are broken gaps in a stone wall which allows free access to predators and enemies. Sometimes we call them "open doors for the enemy". If people are believing lies they will be easy targets. Psalms 91:4 Thy Truth is a shield and buckler (both used for protection from enemies). When people are missing principles of God's Kingdom they have gaps. Can we let Jesus in us fill in those gaps with Truth so people can stand in freedom?

Restore the paths to dwell in

- A path is made from many feet going where they often go. It is the habits of a people; everyday life. Where they live and how they live every day. For many people, there was once a path that their people dwelled in but they lost their way; like many of our dear Native Americans. For other people, It is hard to live without enough food, water, or resources. The 3 mile hike for water every morning to the muddy river in Nigeria made a path. The large commercial well which now serves over 10,000 people has shortened that path and the water doesn't make them sick. They now know there is a God in heaven that cares about them.
- Restoring broken people, families, villages and communities is close to Father God's heart. Poor Health and nutrition shortens the path of a mother's life, her children will have to raise themselves. For people to live and thrive Jesus wants to bring them agriculture, sanitation, clean water, health and hygiene, small businesses, education, and community development.
- God wants a people who can live in His presence and walk in His ways of righteousness and bring His Kingdom to "all tribes and peoples and tongues".

> *Thou wilt show me the path of life: in thy presence is fullness of joy; at thy right hand there are pleasures for evermore.*

He restores my soul: he leads me in the paths of righteousness for his name's sake.

PSALMS 23:3

LIGHT, HEALTH, RIGHTEOUSNESS, GLORY: THIS IS THE HERITAGE OF THE PEOPLE OF ISAIAH 58

Then shall thy light break forth as the morning, and thine health shall spring forth speedily: and thy righteousness shall go before thee; the glory of the LORD shall be thy rereward. Then shalt thou call, and the LORD shall answer; thou shalt cry, and he shall say, Here I am. then shall thy light rise in obscurity, and thy darkness be as the noonday:

ISAIAH 58:8-10

And the LORD shall guide thee continually, and satisfy thy soul in drought, and make fat thy bones: and thou shalt be like a watered garden, and like a spring of water, whose waters fail not.

ISAIAH 58:11

Then shalt thou delight thyself in the LORD; and
I will cause thee to ride upon the high places
of the earth, and feed thee with the heritage
of Jacob thy father: for the mouth of the
LORD hath spoken it.

ISAIAH 58:14

- God declares through Isaiah that we will be like a watered garden, fully satisfied and never dry.
- God declared we would be delighted in Him, He would guide us continually: We will never lack for His good direction.
- God declared that we would be full of light like mid-day. That we would rise up and our light would be seen by many. (read **Isaiah 60**)
- God said that He would feed us with what He promised Jacob.
- God said then we would ride on the high places of the earth... with Him

His own mouth declared prosperity, blessing, favor in high places, favor with God, and spiritual experiences with God. All God really means by this can only be reached by learning to go lower and serve better and love stronger and believe more... FOR OTHERS

FOR THE MOUTH OF THE LORD HAS SPOKEN IT

This is one chapter that the Lord personally "signed" His Name to.

This phrase is only used 4 times in the entire bible.

These promises are endorsed by Him.

All Heaven stands behind these words to perform them.

REVIEW: IMPACT OF ISAIAH 58

1. The prophet Isaiah had to lift up his voice like a trumpet because:
a. People lived far apart
b. They could not hear what God was saying to them
c. They lived in the mountains
d. Their neighbors played loud music

2. God will always hear us when we fast, seek His face and worship
a. True
b. False

3. "You fast for strife a debate refers to:
a. A "look at me" attitude
b. Pride and competition between God's leaders
c. Being willing to fight to be right
d. All of the above

4. How are bands of wickedness broken?

a. Living a fasted lifestyle

b. Praying Louder and longer

c. Lifting weights

d. Sitting in ashes and wearing sackcloth

5. Feeding the hungry in Isaiah 58:6 only means to preach at others

a. True

b. False

6. Caring for your own flesh means

a. Brushing your teeth before meeting people

b. Taking care of your own family with God's love

c. Having compassion for others

d. Getting enough sleep at night

7. We can honor the Sabbath by

a. Not eating on that day

b. Attending several church services

c. Delighting to do His will and speak His words

d. Resting extra on that day

8. Doing deeds of kindness in practical ways can have great spiritual results

a. True

b. False

9. What are breaches?

a. small insects in the water

b. leather straps which attach a warrior's armor

c. boldly colored circles used for target practice

d. gaps of truth in people's lives which allow access to enemies

10. Restoring the Paths to Dwell in

a. Helping broken families and communities to recover and thrive

b. Building houses on the main roads

c. Installing new stop signs for safety

11. Raise up the Foundations of many generations can mean

a. Giving people a new identity on which to build their future

b. Teaching truths which fill in spiritual gaps

c. Giving your children a good education

d. All of the above

12. Bringing God's Kingdom to a village involves only the spiritual truths and principles.

a. True

b. False

13. In this chapter when we deny our own selves to love others God promises that

a. We will become rich

b. We will be the greatest in His Kingdom

c. We will become like a fruitful garden. Never dry

d. We will have the newest vehicle we claim

14. Isaiah 58 fasting releases what God promised to Jacob

a. True
b. False

15. Who signed his name to the promises in this chapter?
a. Jeremiah
b. Joel
c. God
d. Isaiah

DEVO DAY 6

IMPACT OF ISAIAH 58 IN ACTION

There was a family who lived in our town and had come to our church a few times. They had 4 year old twins and the wife was pregnant with their next child. Work had been steady for the husband, but his income did not cover all their expenses. They began to wonder if God cared for them or if He even existed.

At one of their lowest moments, the gentle nudge of the Holy Spirit came to my heart. He said, "take a box of groceries to this family." I had met them already and knew where they lived. When we met at the door and I shared God's love for them in this practical way, I told them, "This food is God's love for you, please don't thank me, thank Him."

We developed a close relationship that lasted many years, and later they told me that they could barely wait to close the door before they burst into tears of gratitude and repentance for doubting God. As far as I know, they never doubted God's love that way again.

When God blesses people through our hands in practical ways that demonstrate His love and provision, and they open their hearts to talk with Him and thank Him; this opens communication with the Father God. And that leads them to talk often with their God, they learn to turn to Him instead of against Him.

PROPHECY #1

"For surely the Lord saith unto thee this day, this is the day of the Almighty. This is the day when I am going to show my strength, saith God. I shall not hold back any longer, but I shall uphold my servants, I shall show even the world who I am. For yes, they have made light of me, saith God, but I shall laugh at them, saith the Lord. For they shall see the calamity come upon themselves, for they have mocked God. Yea, they have mocked His work, but I say unto thee, my children, I am the Lord and I fail not. And that which I purpose shall come to pass, and no man shall hinder. And it is so, that even as the light is come, the light shall be brighter and brighter until my glory shall fill the earth. And all men shall know that I am the Lord, for surely no man shall stop the Spirit of the Lord. For I shall bring to pass that which I have spoken.

For ye have not spoken it, but I have spoken it saith the Lord, and my word does not fail, but it comes to pass. For if you will follow me, saith God, surely you shall see the kingdom of God come forth, and you shall behold the greater works that man hath not yet seen. But if you will let me prepare your heart, if you will allow me to take from your life these things which have hindered thee, surely thou shalt see the glory of the Lord, and thou shall know the Lord thy God. And thou shalt surely know that the Lord is faithful unto me, saith God. Be not afraid of the things that are coming upon the earth, but know that I am God, that I have heard the cry of the hungry and the cry of the needy, and I shall answer that cry.

So be unto Me that servant that I would have thee to be, and I will direct thee in all thy ways, and I shall lead thee into My ways, saith God. And know of a surety, the light shall be brighter and brighter and I shall walk with thee continually and I will fulfill My Word, and it shall come to pass even as I have spoken it.

Fear not man, but walk thou in the fear of the Lord, and know that the Lord is with thee to keep thee, to bless thee, to use thee that He might be glorified. For surely the Lord shall be glorified in that people who give Him the glory.

Prophesy given through Rev. Agnes I. Numer

PROPHECY #2

"For, behold, the Lord shall have a people, and yea that people shall be a holy people, a righteous people, and He shall bring forth His righteousness and His holiness through these people. And He shall speak His words, and He shall speak them quickly. And yea the truth shall come, and the truth shall make the people free. But if they hear not, the truth, they shall believe lies and they shall go down with the lies. For this is the day of revelation of Jesus Christ unto His people that cry out to know Him, for He shall surely reveal Himself unto them, and they shall know Him, and He shall speak through them words of life and not death... words of truth that will loose the captives and make them free.

Yea, this day the Lord is speaking unto thee, "look not about thee at the circumstances, but look unto the Lord." For surely the Lord shall take thy like and bring His righteousness into you ...and shall flow through them, and the fear of the Lord shall come upon the people. For arise in His people and surely the Lord shall cause the people to know that He is God. Oh, man has thought little of God and thought they could do all things and get by with it, but I say unto you, this is the day when the Lord is taking His strength out of captivity and His glory out of the enemy's hands, and God shall be glorified in a people and they shall glorify Him.

Surely the Lord looketh for that people and desireth to make every one of you that light that would be bright in this world of darkness. Hear the word of the Lord this morning and hold not back, but hear the word of the Lord, for God would use thee, yea, in a mighty way, if you will let Him flow through you to accomplish His purpose. Even this hour, saith the Lord, you shall begin to see the hand of God move in ways that you've never known. So be not in doubt and unbelief, but give glory unto God and know that it is not man, but it is the Lord. Don't doubt in your heart, but believe. If God said it, then God will perform it, for His Word is true and He is faithful and there is nothing too hard for Him to do.

So yea, look unto the Lord with all thy heart and know that the Lord is there to help thee. Hold not back, but give glory unto God, and praise His name, and know of a surety God shall use thee to build up the waste places and use you to lay that foundation and restore places to dwell in. The Lord shall give you the strength that you need, and He will cause you to do it, as you glorify Him, He shall be glorified, and He shall accomplish His purpose. Oh, if man would only believe. All things are possible to him that believeth. So, hold not back, but rejoice in Him and He shall surely bring it to pass. Honor Him in all things. Praise Him in all things and give Him glory. And ye shall surely walk in the light of His presence. And He shall be unto thee that light that shall never fail. Thank you Lord.

Prophesy given through Rev. Agnes I. Numer

ANSWER KEY

THE BEATITUDES

Which Beatitude is missing?

Answer: Blessed are the meek.

REVIEW: LORD, YOU HAVE ORDAINED PEACE FOR US

1. False

2. c. Accepting the peace God offers us

3. a. Renouncing them

4. c. Receive the truth

5. b. God's word is in us, and He is the one that keeps us from fear

6. True

7. False

8. c. We dig up the past or we live in sin

9. True

10. False

REVIEW: CONFLICT REVOLUTION

1. a. A conflict

2. True

3. True

4. d. All of the above

5. False

6. any of the below

a. Allow deep sympathy for the person to invade your heart

b. Let God heal you from past issues which arise in present conflicts

c. Learn to love with God's love

d. Realize how habits and addictions are affecting your relationships

7. c. The vows you make

8. False

9. True

10. False

11. False

12. Choose 4 words which define unconditional love

a. Wholehearted

c. Unrestricted

d. Unlimited

g. Unreserved

13. False

14. Choose 4 points to argue fairly

b. Listen respectfully

c. Stay to the point. Don't get sidetracked

f. Respond, don't react

g. Don't argue when angry

15. c. I am sorry, I was wrong

16. d. God's

REVIEW: PRAISE AND WORSHIP

1. True

2. False

3. True

4. guard; presence; healing; restoration

5. pure; heart; shame

6. Yes

7. True

8. False

9. chose; strengthens

10. Soulish Realm

11. d. All the above

12. c. Play with confidence in yourself as a great musician

13. compliment; expect; assist

14. b. Yell at the congregation

QUIZ: SPIRITUAL WARFARE

1. True

2. God is not for us – we are for Him

3. True

4. False

5. False

6. a. Do not move in presumption

7. d. All of the above

8. True

9. True

10. d. All of the above

11. True

12. True

13. d. All of the above

14. b. To disown, repent or walk away

15. True

REVIEW: ISAIAH 58

1. b. They could not hear what God was saying to them

2. True

3. d. All of the above

4. Living a fasted lifestyle

5. False

6. c. Having compassion for others

7. c. Delighting to do His will and speak His words

8. True

9. d. gaps of truth in people's lives which allow access to enemies

10. a. Helping broken families and communities to recover and thrive

11. d. All of the above

12. False

13. c. We will become like a fruitful garden. Never dry

14. True

15. c. God

NOTES

DEVO DAY 1

1. **Kingdom:**
   Strong's Definitions: βασιλεία **basileía**, bas-il-i'-ah; from G935; properly, royalty, i.e. (abstractly) rule, or (concretely) a realm (literally or figuratively):—kingdom, + reign.
   Outline of Biblical Usage
   1 royal power, kingship, dominion, rule
   1 not to be confused with an actual kingdom but rather the right or authority to rule over a kingdom
   2 of the royal power of Jesus as the triumphant Messiah
   3 of the royal power and dignity conferred on Christians in the Messiah's kingdom
   2 a kingdom, the territory subject to the rule of a king
   3 used in the N.T. to refer to the reign of the Messiah

2. **Heaven:**
   Strong's Definitions: οὐρανός **ouranós**, oo-ran-os'; perhaps from the same as G3735 (through the idea of elevation); the sky; by extension, heaven (as the abode of God); by implication, happiness, power, eternity; specially, the Gospel (Christianity):—air, heaven(-ly), sky.
   Outline of Biblical Usage:
   1 the vaulted expanse of the sky with all things visible in it 1 the universe, the world
   2 the aerial heavens or sky, the region where the clouds and the tempests gather, and where thunder and lightning are produced
   3 the sidereal or starry heavens
   2 the region above the sidereal heavens, the seat of order of things eternal and consummately perfect where God dwells and other heavenly beings

3. **shall be comforted:**
   Strong's Definitions: παρακαλέω **parakaléō**, par-ak-al-eh'-o; from G3844 and G2564; to call near, i.e. invite, invoke (by imploration, hortation or consolation):—beseech, call for, (be of good) comfort, desire, (give) exhort(-ation), intreat, pray.
   Outline of Biblical Usage:
   1   to call to one's side, call for, summon

2   to address, speak to, (call to, call upon), which may be done in the way of exhortation, entreaty, comfort, instruction, etc.

1   to admonish, exhort

2   to beg, entreat, beseech

1   to strive to appease by entreaty

3   to console, to encourage and strengthen by consolation, to comfort

1   to receive consolation, be comforted

4   to encourage, strengthen

5   exhorting and comforting and encouraging

6   to instruct, teach

4. **shall inherit:**

Strong's Definitions: κληρονομέω **klēronoméō**, klay-ron-om-eh'-o; from G2818; to be an heir to (literally or figuratively):—be heir, (obtain by) inherit(-ance).

Outline of Biblical Usage:

1 to receive a lot, receive by lot

1 esp. to receive a part of an inheritance, receive as an inheritance, obtain by right of inheritance

2 to be an heir, to inherit

2 to receive the portion assigned to one, receive an allotted portion, receive as one's own or as a possession

3 to become partaker of, to obtain

5. **filled:**

Strong's Definitions: χορτάζω **chortázō**, khor-tad'-zo; from G5528; to fodder, i.e. (generally) to gorge (supply food in abundance):—feed, fill, satisfy.

Outline of Biblical Usage:

1 to feed with herbs, grass, hay, to fill, satisfy with food, to fatten

1 of animals

2 to fill or satisfy men

3 to fulfil or satisfy the desire of any one

6. **obtain mercy:**

Strong's Definitions: ἐλεέω **eleéō**, el-eh-eh'-o; from G1656; to compassionate (by word or deed, specially, by divine grace):—have compassion (pity on), have (obtain, receive, shew) mercy (on).

Outline of Biblical Usage:

1 to have mercy on

2 to help one afflicted or seeking aid

3 to help the afflicted, to bring help to the wretched

4 to experience mercy

7. **pure:**

Strong's Definitions: καθαρός **katharós**, kath-ar-os'; of uncertain affinity; clean (literally or figuratively):—clean, clear, pure.

Outline of Biblical Usage:

1 clean, pure

1 physically

1 purified by fire

2 in a similitude, like a vine cleansed by pruning and so fitted to bear fruit

2 in a levitical sense

1 clean, the use of which is not forbidden, imparts no uncleanness

3 ethically

1 free from corrupt desire, from sin and guilt

2 free from every admixture of what is false, sincere genuine

3 blameless, innocent

4 unstained with the guilt of anything

8. **in heart:**

Strong's Definitions: καρδία **kardía**, kar-dee'-ah; prolonged from a primary κάρ kár (Latin cor, "heart"); the heart, i.e. (figuratively) the thoughts or feelings (mind); also (by analogy) the middle:—(+ broken-)heart(-ed).

the heart

Outline of Biblical Usage:

1 that organ in the animal body which is the centre of the circulation of the blood, and hence was regarded as the seat of physical life

2 denotes the centre of all physical and spiritual life

1 the vigour and sense of physical life

2 the centre and seat of spiritual life

1 the soul or mind, as it is the fountain and seat of the thoughts, passions, desires, appetites, affections, purposes, endeavours

2 of the understanding, the faculty and seat of the intelligence

3 of the will and character

4 of the soul so far as it is affected and stirred in a bad way or good, or of the soul as the seat of the sensibilities, affections, emotions, desires, appetites, passions

3 of the middle or central or inmost part of anything, even though inanimate

9. **see:**

Strong's Definitions: ὀπτάνομαι **optánomai**, op-tan'-om-ahee; a (middle voice) prolonged form of the primary (middle voice) ὄπτομαι óptomai op'-tom-ahee; which is used for it in certain tenses; and both as alternate of G3708; to gaze (i.e. with wide-open eyes, as at something remarkable; and thus differing from G991, which denotes simply voluntary observation; and from G1492, which expresses merely mechanical, passive or casual vision; while G2300, and still more emphatically its intensive G2334, signifies an earnest but more continued inspection; and G4648 a watching from a distance):—appear, look, see, shew self.

Outline of Biblical Usage:
1 to look at, behold
2 to allow one's self to be seen, to appear

10. **God:**

Strong's Definitions: θεός theós, theh'-os; of uncertain affinity; a deity, especially (with G3588) the supreme Divinity; figuratively, a magistrate; by Hebraism, very:—X exceeding, God, god(-ly, -ward).

Outline of Biblical Usage:
1 a god or goddess, a general name of deities or divinities
2 the Godhead, trinity
1 God the Father, the first person in the trinity
2 Christ, the second person of the trinity
3 Holy Spirit, the third person in the trinity
3 spoken of the only and true God
1 refers to the things of God
2 his counsels, interests, things due to him
4 whatever can in any respect be likened unto God, or resemble him in any way
1 God's representative or viceregent
1 of magistrates and judges

11. **children:**

Strong's Definitions: υἱός huiŏs, hwee-os'; apparently a primary word; a "son" (sometimes of animals), used very widely of immediate, remote or figuratively, kinship:—child, foal, son.

Outline of Biblical Usage:
1 a son
1 rarely used for the young of animals
2 generally used of the offspring of men
3 in a restricted sense, the male offspring (one born by a father and of a mother)
4 in a wider sense, a descendant, one of the posterity of any one,
1 the children of Israel
2 sons of Abraham
5 used to describe one who depends on another or is his follower
1 a pupil

12. **righteousness' sake:**

Strong's Definitions: δικαιοσύνη dikaiosýnē, dik-ah-yos-oo'-nay;

from G1342; equity (of character or act); specially (Christian) justification:—righteousness.

Outline of Biblical Usage:

1 in a broad sense: state of him who is as he ought to be, righteousness, the condition acceptable to God

1 the doctrine concerning the way in which man may attain a state approved of God

2 integrity, virtue, purity of life, rightness, correctness of thinking feeling, and acting

2 in a narrower sense, justice or the virtue which gives each his due

ACKNOWLEDGEMENTS

Special thank you to the artists for the use of the following pictures:

BEATITUDES:

Artist: Larry Cole
- The Love Story

Artists: David Chika Onoh, Jackson Muthoni
- The Beatitudes

Artist: Rebecca Brogan
- Its Time to Go Home Now

LORD, YOU HAVE ORDAINED PEACE FOR US

Artist: Rebecca Brogan
- Jesus my Ransom
- Please Let Me Love Your Pain Away

PRAISE AND WORSHIP

- Through Fire and Water Praise Comes Forth
- The Anointing Series
- Home Is Where Your Heart Is
- The Army of The Lord Advancing

SPIRITUAL WARFARE:

Artist: Rebecca Brogan
- Vindication
- Kept Safe in The Hands of God
- Spiritual Warfare
Artist: Gilbert Dudley
- Armor of Christ Amor of Antichrist

IMPACT OF ISAIAH 58:

Artist: George Thomas
- Love the Family
- Vision of Isaiah 58

Special thanks to Rebecca Brogan - artist
Rebecca Brogan website: www.jtbarts.com

www.ingramcontent.com/pod-product-compliance
Lightning Source LLC
Chambersburg PA
CBHW061158120626
46546CB00005B/2103